Grandma's Cookbook

Recipes inspired by the National Trust

Grandma's Cookbook

Recipes inspired by the National Trust

Laura Mason and Sara Paston-Williams

First published in the United Kingdom in 2012 as
Good Old-fashioned Pies and Stews and *Good Old-fashioned Puddings*
by National Trust Books.

This edition first published in 2013 by
National Trust Books
10 Southcombe Street
London W14 0RA
An imprint of Anova Books Ltd

Text and recipes © Laura Mason and Sara Paston-Williams
Copyright © National Trust Books

ISBN 9781907892691

A CIP catalogue record for this book is available from the British
Library.

20 19 18 17 16 15 14 13
10 9 8 7 6 5 4 3 2 1

Reproduction by Mission, Hong Kong.
Printed by 1010 Printing International Ltd, China

Produced by SP Creative Design
Editor: Heather Thomas
Designer: Rolando Ugolini
Food photography: Tara Fisher
Home economist: Jane Suthering
Food styling: Wei Tang

Warning: recipes containing raw eggs are unsuitable for pregnant
women or young children.

Contents

Introduction

Old-fashioned hearty stews, pies and puddings are comforting dishes, which lift our hearts when we're feeling low, weary or cold. They belong to traditional British cookery, and the delicious recipes have been passed down from one generation to the next. Some are regional country dishes that belong to the classic 'good old plain cooking' tradition with its emphasis on local ingredients, while others are more elegant and refined. Together, they all celebrate the diversity and wonderful heritage of time-honoured British food.

Stews and pies

These dishes tend to use inexpensive cuts of meat and are economical of fuel. What's more, many can be prepared in advance and left in a low oven while the cook does something else, or they can be reheated at a later date. These are quiet and good-tempered dishes. Stews and pies are much more varied than mere chunks of meat and onions in a thick brown gravy. In this book, we have explored other possibilities: unthickened sauces that are light and fresh; a large piece of meat instead of cubes; pies served cold instead of hot. There are also recipes for fish and vegetable stews and pies.

Making stews

Making a basic stew is about harmonising ingredients and developing flavours – allowing tougher cuts of meat to become tender and blending them with a selection of root vegetables into a well-seasoned and pleasing entity.

A good container is essential; all you have to discover is which works best for you. Most people acquire a casserole that becomes a favourite because it cooks food well, holds the right amount for their family's needs and looks good. If you don't have a traditional round cast-iron casserole, a large reasonably heavy pan or deep frying pan with a close-fitting lid will hold a stew for simmering over a low flame (alternatively, it can be put in the oven if it is designed for this, but do remember that the handle will get very hot). The best casseroles are flameproof ones that can be used on the hob as well as in the oven.

One of the best things about stews is their flexibility. You can combine the ingredients, pour them into a casserole, cover and pop into a low oven, and just leave well alone for two to three hours. At the end of this time, you should have a perfectly good dish. To cook stews successfully on the hob, you must take care to keep the liquid just below boiling – only the slightest movement should be apparent on the surface. The simmering plate of an Aga is ideal for this as it provides a really low heat. Of course, if you have a slow cooker, your stew will require even less attention – just follow the manufacturer's instructions.

A cooked meat stew often has a fair amount of excess fat on the surface, either from frying the ingredients in the initial stages or from fat that is given up by the meat during cooking. If serving the stew immediately, remove as much fat as possible by skimming it off with a spoon or blotting the surface with kitchen paper, trying not to pick up any of the sauce in the process. Otherwise, allow the stew to cool and then chill in the refrigerator overnight. The next day, it is easy to lift the solidified fat off the surface.

With the exception of stews made from veal or game birds (in which the meat tends to dryness), most meat stews taste better after reheating the next day, when the flavours have had a chance to mellow and blend. Store cooled stews in a cold larder or the refrigerator overnight, or pour into a suitable container for freezing. Leave any final thickenings or additions, such as breadcrumbs or dumplings, until you are ready to reheat a stew. Those based on vegetables or fish don't reheat well as the fresh flavours and subtle textures are often lost in the process.

A stew that has been cooked and then frozen is best defrosted at room temperature for several hours or overnight before it is needed. Don't worry too much if the sauce appears to separate – it should come back together with a little stirring when the mixture is reheated and hot again.

For reheating, put the mixture into a suitable serving dish. Heat in a preheated moderate oven, 180°C (350°F, Gas mark 4), for about 30 minutes or until piping hot, i.e. not far off boiling, stirring from time to time. If you prefer, you can reheat it in a pan, but watch carefully and stir frequently to make sure the mixture heats evenly and doesn't stick. A little water can be added to thin particularly thick sauces during the process.

Making pies

Pie dishes and plates are widely available. Deep-filled pies require round, oblong or oval pie dishes with wide rims to support the edges of the pastry covering, unless they are to be topped with mashed potato. Pie dishes are usually made of earthenware, glass or enamelled iron and share the various advantages and disadvantages of these materials. Traditional English pie funnels shaped as blackbirds are a nice traditional touch to support the pastry in the centre and allow steam to escape.

Most savoury pies are covered with shortcrust or puff pastry, or topped with mashed potato, which can be flavoured with herbs or mustard. You can make your own pastry or buy it chilled or frozen in blocks or ready-rolled sheets in your local supermarket. Puff pastry takes a considerable amount of time and skill to make, so most modern cooks opt for convenience and buy it instead.

The method for covering a pie is basically the same, whether using shortcrust or puff pastry. Roll out the pastry on a lightly floured surface to just over 5mm (¼in) thick, aiming for a shape roughly equivalent to the dish, but a little larger. From this, cut a strip about 1.5cm (⅝in) wide, long enough to go around the edge of the dish.

Using a pastry brush, dipped in water, wet the edge of the dish all the way round, then stick the pastry strip to it. Trim the rest of the pastry to the size of the top of the dish. Wet the top of the pastry strip, then cover with the rest of the pastry. Press the two layers lightly together with your fingers (shortcrust pastry can be crimped; cut nicks in the edge of puff pastry to scallop the edge). Cut an air vent in the middle or make a hole where the pie funnel is. Gather together any left-over scraps of pastry, re-roll and cut into leaves or other shapes as desired, then wet the reverse side and use to decorate the pie.

Brush the top of the pie lightly with beaten egg or a little cream or milk. Bake shortcrust-covered pies in a preheated oven at 200°C (400°F, Gas mark 6) for about 20 minutes, then reduce the heat to 180°C (350°F, Gas mark 4) to complete the cooking. Puff pastry needs to rise as well as cook through. Start this in a hot oven at 220°C (425°F, Gas mark 7), turning it down to 180°C (350°F, gas mark 4) for the remainder of the cooking time.

Traditional puddings

The British tradition for delicious puddings is centuries old. Pies, trifles, fools, flummeries, betties and tarts have all been served regularly since medieval times. From the earliest recipes, through elaborate Elizabethan and Stuart sweet confections to the elegant eighteenth- and substantial nineteenth-century puddings, a longstanding tradition has evolved which is now an integral part of Britain's culinary heritage.

Almost all British puddings have descended from two medieval dishes: the early cereal 'pottage', which was a kind of porridge with honey, wild fruits, shredded meat or fish added to make it more palatable; and 'frumenty', a milk pudding made from wheat or barley and eaten with milk and honey on festive occasions. Originally, puddings such as brightly coloured spiced jellies, flummeries, syllabubs, various tarts, custards, junkets and fruit dishes formed part of a second or third course of a meal, served alongside chicken and fish dishes.

The enormous variety of puddings and the rapidity with which they were developed in the seventeenth and eighteenth centuries as sugar became cheaper and more available, helped to fill a need for fat and carbohydrates in people's diets, as well as fresh fruit. The puddings of country folk were often made from meal of cheaper local grains, such as oats and barley rather than wheat, but they were just as satisfying.

Growing literacy allowed women to write down their favourite recipes, including regional dishes. Many of the traditional pudding recipes were preserved in rural areas, particularly in large country houses. In towns, specialty restaurants, gentlemen's clubs and grill rooms of the more exclusive hotels continued to serve truly British puddings, so many recipes have survived, although not always in their original form. In recent years, British puddings have enjoyed a well-deserved revival, and although some are inclined to be rich and fattening, they are homely and delicious and make a lovely treat. 'Pudding-time' still brings murmurs of delight from guests as they tuck into a syrup sponge or plum crumble. Our traditional puddings are glorious – rich and indulgent and comforting. Naughty? Yes, but oh so nice!

Note:
If you want to be a little less indulgent, yoghurt and crème fraîche can be used instead of cream in most recipes, or half and half.

Vegetarian alternatives:
Vegetarian suet and the vegetarian equivalent of lard can be used wherever a recipe includes suet or lard. In fact, I prefer to use vegetarian suet as it gives a lighter finish. Vegetarian setting agents can also be used in place of gelatine, however you must follow the manufacturer's instructions closely.

Stews

A Welsh Stew

Eliza Acton gave this dish in her book *Modern Cookery for Private Families* (1845). It is recognisably a version of cawl, a soup-like stew of meat and vegetables traditional to Welsh cookery. Acton's version is simple but refined. The better the beef and the stock, the better the end result.

serves
4

about 500g (1lb 2oz) stewing beef,
 trimmed of any gristle and fat,
 and cut into slices about 4cm
 (1½in) square
400ml (14fl oz) beef stock
8 leeks

300g (11oz) small white turnips
 (or use a slice from a large one)
salt and black pepper
pinch of sugar
chopped parsley, to serve

Put the beef and the stock in a medium-sized flameproof casserole and bring to a simmer. Cover and transfer to a moderate oven, 180°C (350°F, Gas mark 4). Allow to cook gently for 1 hour.

Prepare the vegetables: cut the white part off the leeks, trim and wash and cut into slices about 2cm (¾in) long (this will probably leave quite a lot of green, the best of which can be used for soup). Peel the turnips: small ones can be cut into quarters; if using a piece of a large one, cut as if making chips.

After 1 hour, remove the casserole from the oven. The beef should be fairly tender and the stock well flavoured. Add the prepared vegetables, 1 teaspoon salt, pepper to taste and a pinch of sugar. Return to the oven for about 1¼ hours. Stir occasionally during this time. Check the seasoning and divide between soup plates.

Dust each portion with parsley and serve with floury potatoes, boiled or steamed.

Beef à la Mode

Beef à la Mode appeared in cookery books in the first half of the eighteenth century, along with Beef Royale, Beef à la Daube and other obviously French-derived dishes. The recipe was used for large pieces of meat; 2.25–2.7kg (5–6lb) was typically quoted. It can be served hot or cold. You may want to include a pig's foot when cooking this – it will help the juices set to a jelly when cool, so they can be chopped and served along with the meat. I have suggested using brisket – not the most elegant cut but excellently flavoured.

serves 8

about 1.5kg (3lb 4oz) brisket, boned
    and rolled
4–6 anchovy fillets
4 cloves
1 blade of mace
6–8 peppercorns
115g (4oz) bacon, cut into matchsticks
150ml (5fl oz) red wine
300ml (10fl oz) strong beef stock
4–6 small shallots
1 garlic clove, peeled but left whole
a bouquet garni made from a bay leaf,
    rosemary, thyme and basil
250g (9oz) carrots, trimmed, peeled
    and cut into quarters lengthways
1 pig's foot, cut into half lengthways
    (optional)
salt and black pepper

Prepare the beef by unrolling; snip the strings tying it if necessary. Distribute the anchovy fillets over the inside. Pound the spices to a powder and sprinkle over the top. Re-roll and tie again with the seasonings inside.

Take a flameproof casserole that will hold the meat snugly. Add the bacon and let it cook gently until the fat runs. Add the wine and bring to the boil. Put in the meat, stock, shallots, garlic and bouquet garni and bring to a simmer. Add the carrots and the pig's foot, if using. Season with 1 teaspoon salt and some pepper.

Cover tightly with doubled greaseproof paper or foil and then the lid of the casserole. Transfer to a preheated low oven, 140°C (275°F, Gas mark 1), and cook for 4 hours. The meat will benefit from being turned once or twice, but it isn't absolutely necessary.

At the end of the cooking time, remove the meat and vegetables to a warm serving dish. Discard the bouquet garni (and the pig's foot, if used). Skim all the fat off the cooking juices. Serve hot with a purée of potato and parsnip to soak up the liquid.

If serving cold: remove the beef, allow it to cool, then store in a cold place; it is better not to refrigerate it unless you have no alternative. Strain the cooking juices, then boil to reduce them by about one-quarter. Pour into a bowl, chill and lift off the fat when cold. Remove the strings, carve the meat into neat slices and garnish with the jelly, chopped into pieces.

Goulash

Goulash was probably introduced to the British repertoire in the early twentieth century. This is based on a version that was regularly made by my mother, who came across it as a child when she lived in Bradford, a city with a significant population of immigrants from Eastern Europe between the world wars. She served it with mashed potatoes or rice, but I prefer pasta.

serves
4

60g (2¼oz) bacon, rind removed, cut into matchsticks
1 medium onion, finely sliced
20g (¾oz) lard
1 garlic clove, crushed
450–500g (1lb–1lb 2oz) stewing beef, trimmed and cut into cubes
1 generous tablespoon paprika

1 teaspoon smoked paprika (optional)
400g (14oz) canned chopped tomatoes
salt
hot buttered noodles or pappardelle, to serve
sour cream, to serve

Fry the bacon until the fat runs in a flameproof casserole dish. Remove the bacon and set aside. Add the onions to the bacon fat together with a little lard if the bacon hasn't yielded much fat. Let the onions cook very slowly until they are quite soft and beginning to turn golden. Add the garlic, cook for 1–2 minutes, then drain with a slotted spoon and set aside with the bacon.

Add any remaining lard, turn up the heat and add the beef. Cook it quite fast, stirring frequently, and when the cubes are browned on all sides, sprinkle in the paprika and the smoked paprika (if using). Cook for 2 more minutes, stirring all the time, then add the cooked bacon and onions. Stir in the tomatoes and add a good pinch of salt. Cover tightly and allow to simmer gently for 1½–2 hours.

At the end of the cooking time, taste the goulash and add more salt if desired. Spoon each portion over some buttered noodles or papardelle and add a spoonful of sour cream to the top. Perhaps not very authentic but good.

Beef Stew with Root Vegetables & Dumplings

This stew has been a mainstay of English domestic cookery since the mid-nineteenth century. Make it with whatever cut of beef you prefer, cook it with stock or beer, and add root vegetables and dumplings – comfort food for the coldest winter day.

serves
4

55g (2oz) beef dripping, lard or oil, plus a little extra
1 large onion, sliced
2 garlic cloves, crushed
140g (5oz) turnip, diced
1 large parsnip, cubed
1 large carrot, cubed
40g (1½oz) flour
450–500g (1lb–1lb 2oz) stewing beef, cut into cubes
250ml (9fl oz) beef stock
250ml (9fl oz) mild beer (optional; use beef stock or wine instead if desired)
1 bay leaf
few sprigs of marjoram, or 1 teaspoon dried marjoram or oregano
salt and black pepper

for the dumplings
1 quantity suet dumpling mix (see page 215) flavoured with horseradish, or mustard and parsley

Heat the dripping, lard or oil in a frying pan or casserole. Fry the onion until translucent, then add the garlic and let it cook a little longer. Remove the mixture from the fat and keep on one side. Fry the root vegetables for a few minutes, then add them to the onions.

Mix 1 teaspoon salt with some pepper and a little of the flour and toss the beef into it. Brown the meat in the remaining fat (in batches if necessary – don't overcrowd the pan). Add the meat to the vegetables in the casserole.

Sprinkle the remaining seasoned flour into the frying pan and stir to make a roux (add a little extra fat first if necessary). Add the beef stock, stirring well and scraping any bits of sediment off the base of the pan. Stir in the beer, if using, and bring to the boil. Pour over the meat and vegetables, add the bay leaf and marjoram, then cover. Cook in a gentle preheated oven, 150°C (300°F, Gas mark 2), for about 2 hours.

Make up the dumpling mix, as described on page 235.

Remove the casserole from the oven and skim off any excess fat. Check the seasoning and add more salt and pepper if necessary. Distribute the dumplings over the top. Turn the heat up to 180°C (350°F, Gas mark 4) and return the dish, uncovered, to the oven for about 20 minutes, or until the dumplings are cooked through and starting to crisp slightly on top.

Adapt the recipe as desired. If using cuts, such as shin of beef or oxtail, reduce the oven temperature to 140°C (275°F, Gas mark 1), and cook for about 4 hours.

Lobscouse with Mustard & Parsley Dumplings

Lobscouse is a type of stew made around the coasts of north-west Europe, including the port of Liverpool. And yes, that's why Liverpudlians became known as scousers. Beef, fresh or salted, is the most usual principal ingredient, although fish versions are also known. Dumplings are a good, if non-traditional, addition. Tender summer carrots, small white turnips and new potatoes are specified for this summer version; winter vegetables, if cubed, will work equally well but they give a more robust flavour.

serves
4

500g (1lb 2oz) good-quality
   braising steak
200g (7oz) young carrots, halved
   lengthways
200g (7oz) small white turnips, cut
   into batons
4 garlic cloves, peeled
bouquet garni of 1 bay leaf, 1 sprig
   rosemary and a few sprigs thyme

300–400ml (10–14fl oz) water
800g (1lb 12oz) new potatoes, scrubbed
salt and black pepper

for the dumplings
1 quantity dumpling mix (see page 215)
1 teaspoon mustard powder
pinch cayenne pepper
1 generous tablespoon chopped parsley

Trim the meat of any obvious fat and gristle, and cut it into 2cm (¾in) cubes. Spread the carrots, turnips and garlic cloves in a layer over the base of a large pan. Tuck the bunch of herbs in among them. Add the beef in a layer on top. Pour in enough water to cover the vegetables and add the salt and some pepper. Cover tightly with a layer of foil under the lid and put on the lowest heat.

Simmer gently for 1 hour, making sure the liquid doesn't boil away. Then uncover the stew, add the potatoes (cut into halves or quarters if they are large), cover the stew again and continue cooking for about 20 minutes.

Towards the end of cooking, make the dumplings, mixing the mustard, cayenne and parsley into the flour. Uncover the stew, remove the bouquet garni, taste the liquid and add more seasoning if necessary. Drop the dumplings on top of the mixture, re-cover and simmer for another 20 minutes.

Stewed Steak

There are many recipes for stewing or braising steak in English cookery books. They are similar in that they rely on combinations of store-cupboard ingredients – beer, vinegar and ready-made sauces, such as Worcestershire sauce or mushroom ketchup – to produce a strongly flavoured gravy. This is an updated version, which includes a currently fashionable ingredient in the form of balsamic vinegar (but use an inexpensive vinegar, not the costly and precious type). This dish shares the characteristics of similar recipes from the past in that it is quick and simple to put together and nice to eat, especially on a cold day.

serves
4

about 500g (1lb 2oz) braising steak,
    cut into slices about 2cm (¾in) thick
4 garlic cloves, peeled
1 piece of star anise
4 tablespoons soy sauce
2 tablespoons balsamic vinegar
200ml (7fl oz) tomato juice

Put the steak in a shallow ovenproof dish along with the garlic and star anise. Mix together the other ingredients and pour over the top. Cover the dish with foil and then with a lid if the dish has one.

Cook in a preheated low oven, 140°C (275°F, Gas mark 1), for 3 hours, by which time the meat should be extremely tender and surrounded by a well-flavoured sauce. Serve with a mixture of potato and parsnip mashed together.

Braised Ox Cheek
with Wine, Cloves & Oranges

Ox cheek is cheap and well flavoured but needs gentle cooking. This recipe also works with braising steak or escalopes if preferred; shorten the cooking time accordingly. In *The Accomplisht Cook* (1685) Robert May gave a recipe for 'stewed collops of beef', which was the inspiration here and an ancestor of all those dishes of steak braised with wine, beer or the highly seasoned sauces made by commercial sauce manufacturers in the nineteenth century. The key is strong beef stock: use a home-made one if possible, or a good ready-made one, and reduce it to concentrate the flavour. Really good gravy left from a roast of beef could also be used.

serves
4

600–700g (1lb 5oz–1lb 9oz) ox cheek,
cut to give 3–4 thick slices from
each one
220ml (8fl oz) red wine
150ml (5fl oz) well-flavoured
beef stock

1 orange
6 cloves
scrape of nutmeg
20g (¾oz) flour
20g (¾oz) butter
salt and black pepper

Put the ox cheek in a shallow ovenproof dish. Mix the wine and stock in a small pan. Remove 4–5 strips of zest from the orange with a canelle knife or potato peeler and add them, along with the cloves and a generous scrape of nutmeg, to the pan. Grind in a little black pepper, add about ½ teaspoon salt, and bring the mixture to a simmer. Pour over the beef, then cover tightly with foil and the lid of the dish if it has one.

Cook in a low preheated oven, 140°C (275°F, Gas mark 1) or lower, if possible, for 3–3½ hours. Remove the meat to a warm serving dish. Add the juice of half the orange, or more to taste, plus extra salt and pepper as desired.

Knead the flour and butter together and dot over the surface of the sauce, shaking the dish so that it melts into the liquid. The sauce may need to be briefly reheated but don't overdo it – just enough to thicken it lightly. Serve with a very creamy purée of potato or some plain steamed potatoes.

If using braising steak, it can be cooked for a shorter time at a higher temperature – 1½–2 hours at 150°C (300°F, Gas mark 2).

Ragoût of Oxtail

2 oxtails, cut into pieces
1 medium onion, finely chopped
2 garlic cloves, crushed
2 bay leaves, spines removed,
   the remainder finely shredded
1 generous tablespoon chopped parsley
leaves of 3–4 sprigs fresh thyme
600ml (1 pint) red wine
200g (7oz) unsmoked pancetta or
   good bacon, diced

250g (9oz) carrot, diced
250g (9oz) mushrooms, finely sliced
1 generous tablespoon truffle paste
   (optional)
500g (1lb 2oz) shallots, peeled
425ml (15fl oz) beef stock
40g (1½oz) flour
40g (1½oz) butter
salt and black pepper

Dissolve 1 tablespoon salt in cold water, then soak the oxtail pieces in it for about 1 hour. Drain well. Put the pieces of oxtail into a deep bowl. Mix the chopped onion, garlic, bay leaves, parsley, thyme, a generous quantity of pepper and the wine, and pour over the meat. Cover and leave to marinate for at least 4 hours.

When ready to cook the stew, take a large flameproof casserole and set it over a low heat. Add the pancetta or bacon to the casserole and cook until starting to crisp. Put the carrot and mushrooms on top (no need to stir) and add the truffle paste, if using. Then add the pieces of oxtail in a layer, and tuck the shallots into the spaces between them.

Pour over the marinade, turn up the heat and let it bubble. Add the beef stock and 1 generous teaspoon salt. Bring to the boil, skim off any scum on the surface, then cover the casserole with foil and the lid, and put in a preheated low oven, 140°C (275°F, Gas mark 1). Leave strictly alone for 4 hours.

At the end of the cooking time, remove from the oven and skim off as much fat as possible. Taste and correct the seasoning. Knead the flour and butter together to make a *beurre manié* and dot small pieces of this over the surface of the liquid (remove the pieces of oxtail to a hot serving dish if they seem to be in the way). Heat gently and stir until the sauce has thickened.

Serve with mashed potato, or a purée of potato and celeriac.

Spring Stew of Veal

In summer, many English cooks liked to pair veal with fresh greenery and slightly acid flavours. Sorrel was often chosen, but this more unusual combination of cucumber, gooseberries and lettuce was suggested by Eliza Acton in 1845. She cooked everything together from the start, but the vegetables become very soft this way. However, put them in about halfway through cooking, as below, and they retain a little texture.

serves 4

450–500g (1lb–1lb 2oz) stewing veal, cut into 2cm (¾in) cubes
25g (1oz) flour
40g (1½oz) butter
6 spring onions, trimmed and cut into 2cm (¾in) lengths
150g (5oz) green gooseberries
350ml (12fl oz) veal or chicken stock

½ cucumber, peeled, seeds removed and flesh cut into 1cm (½in) dice
2 Little Gem lettuces, outer leaves removed, trimmed, washed and cut into quarters lengthways
salt and black pepper
snipped chives, to garnish

Toss the veal in the flour. Melt the butter in a frying pan or flameproof casserole. Add the veal and fry briskly to brown. Add the spring onions and gooseberries and continue frying for a few minutes. Stir in any remaining flour, then add the stock, stirring well to make a sauce. Add ½ teaspoon salt and a little pepper. Cover well and simmer gently for about 1 hour, stirring occasionally.

Add the cucumber and lettuce. Cover and cook for 1 hour, or until the meat is tender and the vegetables are cooked. Stir, check the seasoning, and garnish with a scattering of snipped chives. Serve with new potatoes.

Veal Olives

These thinly rolled slices of veal were sometimes used as pie fillings in the seventeenth and eighteenth centuries, but they are very good on their own with a little sauce. The name has nothing to do with olives but is derived from an old French word for lark: the little meat rolls, plumply stuffed, are reminiscent of small birds lying in the dish.

Mace, a popular spice in the eighteenth century, is best bought whole; crush it to a powder with a mortar and pestle just before using. The recipe can be used with beef olives as well – omit the Parma ham and use red wine and beef stock as the cooking liquids.

serves
4

4 veal escalopes, each weighing
    approximately 100g (3½oz)
2 slices Parma ham
100g (3½oz) breadcrumbs
55g (2oz) butter, plus a little extra
    for frying
2 anchovies
leaves of 3–4 sprigs thyme

zest of ½ lemon, finely grated
about ½ teaspoon ground mace
1 small egg, beaten
200g (7oz) button mushrooms,
    trimmed and sliced
125ml (4fl oz) dry sherry
125ml (4fl oz) veal or chicken stock
salt and black pepper

Place the escalopes on a plate or board and cover each one with a slice of Parma ham. Put the breadcrumbs in a bowl. Melt the butter and crush the anchovies into it. Pour into the breadcrumbs, then add the thyme, lemon, mace and some black pepper. Mix in the egg and stir well. Divide into 4 portions and spread each one over the ham on top of the escalopes. Roll up, enclosing the stuffing, and tie each olive with thread in two or three places.

Melt a little butter in a flameproof casserole dish and fry the olives briefly, just enough to brown them lightly. Remove to a plate, and add the sliced mushrooms to the dish. Fry, stirring well, until they brown a little. Put the rolls of meat back in, pour in the sherry and let it bubble, then add the stock and bring to a simmer.

Cover the dish and transfer to a preheated moderate oven, 150°C (300°F, Gas mark 2) for 1 hour. Serve with plain boiled rice.

Harrico of Mutton or Lamb

The word haricot (or harrico) is derived from French *harigoter* ('to cut up'). It meant a stew or ragoo but got confused with the usage of haricot as a name for beans in French, and sometimes led English cooks to think that haricot of mutton included beans. This summery version doesn't, but by all means add some fresh French beans towards the end of the cooking time.

This recipe is based on one given by Anne Cobbett in her book *The English Housekeeper* (1851). She evidently considered the basic recipe bland and added proprietary sauces popular in the mid-nineteenth century. I've suggested Thai fish sauce, which adds a salty note. For the stock, use lamb or chicken stock, simmered with turnip, carrot, onion and parsley to strengthen the flavour.

serves
4

500–600g (1lb 2oz–1lb 5oz) lamb
    or mutton – best end of neck,
    loin or chump chops
25g (1oz) butter
400ml (14fl oz) strong stock
4–6 small young carrots, cut into
    quarters lengthways
a bunch of spring onions, cut into
    3–4cm (1¼–1½in) lengths
200g (7oz) small white turnips or
    kohlrabi, peeled and cut into sticks

4 celery stalks, cut into 3–4cm
    (1¼–1½in) lengths
15g (½oz) flour
salt and black pepper

to season (optional)
cayenne pepper
Worcestershire sauce
nam pla (Thai fish sauce)

Trim the chops of any excessive fat. Melt half the butter in a large frying pan and brown the chops on both sides. Add the stock, bring to the boil and simmer gently for 45 minutes. Add the vegetables and cook gently for 15–20 minutes by which time, the meat should be tender. Season carefully. A pinch of cayenne, following Anne Cobbett's example, is a good addition, as are about 1 teaspoon of each of the sauces. If using these, remember that they are salty, and add them before finally tasting and adding any more salt and pepper.

Knead the remaining butter with the flour and drop into the stew in small pieces. Heat gently until boiling, shaking to distribute the butter through the liquid, so that the sauce thickens. Serve with new potatoes and other vegetables as desired.

Irish Stew

This is comfort food – a simple, inexpensive dish known in the cookery of Ireland and Britain since at least the mid-nineteenth century. Irish Stew was originally made in a pan, cooked gently on top of the stove, and often considered better if some of the potatoes began to dissolve into the mixture, thickening it. The best stews were said to be made with the minimum of water or stock. Cooking in the oven means it can be left to look after itself – but you can put it in a pan and simmer on the very lowest heat on the hob if preferred. It has a gentle, mild flavour; if you find it bland, try adding the mixture suggested at the end.

serves 4

300g (11oz) onion, coarsely chopped
1kg (2lb 4oz) neck of lamb (middle or scrag), cut into chops
300g (11oz) small white turnips, halved and cut into slices lengthways
1.2kg (2lb 11oz) potatoes, cut into large dice
salt and black pepper

300ml (10fl oz) stock (lamb for preference)

to garnish (optional)
a handful of fresh coriander leaves
1 small garlic clove, peeled
1 fresh hot green chilli, to taste
a little finely grated lemon zest

Take a large casserole (or pan) and build the meat and vegetables in layers, beginning with the onion and following with the meat, turnips and potatoes, then repeating until the ingredients are used up. Sprinkle a teaspoon of salt and some pepper between the layers. Bring the stock to the boil, pour over the meat and vegetables and cover with buttered foil or paper and the lid.

Cook in a preheated oven, 180°C (350°F, Gas mark 4), for at least 2 hours, or longer on a lower temperature, if desired. A stew simmering on the hob will need checking occasionally to make sure it isn't drying out.

At the end of cooking, taste, correct the seasoning, and serve straight from the pot. To garnish, chop the coriander leaves, garlic and green chilli fairly finely, stir in the lemon zest and scatter a little of this mixture over each portion.

Lamb Meatballs

Recipes for meatballs appear in early English recipe books from the end of the sixteenth until the middle of the eighteenth century. They were highly seasoned and enhanced with whatever spices, dried fruit and nuts happened to be fashionable at the time. This version is loosely based on recipes from the early eighteenth century.

serves
4

400g (14oz) minced lamb
55g (2oz) fresh white breadcrumbs
1 garlic clove, crushed
1 tablespoon very finely chopped
    parsley
1 tablespoon finely chopped basil
½ teaspoon nutmeg
1 egg, beaten
30g (1oz) pistachio nuts, blanched
    (optional)

2 rashers fatty bacon (unsmoked),
    diced
10–12 small shallots, peeled
150ml (5fl oz) red wine
150ml (5fl oz) good stock,
    beef for preference
2 teaspoons cornflour, slaked
    with a little water
salt and black pepper

Put the lamb, breadcrumbs, garlic, herbs, nutmeg, 1 teaspoon salt, pepper to taste, and the beaten egg in a large bowl. Mix well – this task is best done by kneading everything together by hand.

Divide the mixture into 20 pieces and form each one into a small ball (wet your hands in cold water to stop it sticking). If using pistachio nuts, seal one or two in the centre of each little ball. Heat a deep frying pan or shallow flameproof casserole and add the bacon pieces. Fry gently until they have yielded most of their fat. Add the peeled shallots and the meatballs and let them cook gently, turning occasionally, until the meatballs have browned on all sides.

Pour in the wine and let it bubble, then add the stock. Cover and cook gently for 30–45 minutes. Stir in the cornflour mixture, heating gently and stirring all the time until the sauce thickens. Taste and correct the seasoning if necessary. Serve with plain boiled rice or mashed potato and a salad of bitter leaves.

Bolton Hotpot

serves
4

oysters – as many as you like or can
    afford, up to 20 (optional)
55g (2oz) beef dripping
1 large onion, thinly sliced
2 garlic cloves, crushed
800g–1kg (1lb 12oz–2lb 4oz) middle
    neck of lamb, cut into chops
25g (1oz) flour

400ml (14fl oz) stock, preferably lamb,
2 lamb's kidneys, cored and
    cut into slices
pinch of ground allspice
250g (9oz) mushrooms, thinly sliced
900g (2lb) potatoes, peeled and sliced
a little butter
salt and black pepper

If using oysters, open them first, or ask the fishmonger to do so. Strain and
reserve any liquor they contain to remove any stray bits of shell or grit.

Melt the dripping in a frying pan and add the onion. Cook briskly until it starts to
turn golden. Add the garlic, stir well, cook for a moment longer, then drain and
remove the onion to a large deep casserole or other ovenproof dish. Put the chops
into the hot fat and brown on both sides, then put them on top of the onion.

Sprinkle the flour into the fat left in the pan and stir to make a *roux*. Stir in the
heated stock to make a sauce. Add 1 generous teaspoon salt and plenty of pepper.
Allow it to cook gently for a few minutes. Put the kidneys on top of the chops
and dust them with a little allspice. Next add the sliced mushrooms in a layer,
then the oysters, if you are using them. Add the oyster liquor if there is any, and
pour over the sauce from the frying pan. Put the potatoes on top, ending with a
nice neat layer of large overlapping slices. Dot with small pieces of butter.

Cover with the lid of the casserole and cook in a preheated oven, 180°C (350°F,
Gas mark 4), for about 2½ hours. Then uncover the dish, turn the heat up to
200°C (400°F, Gas mark 6), and cook for another 20 minutes or so to brown the
top layer of potatoes.

Pickled red cabbage is the traditional accompaniment to hotpot in Lancashire.

Lamb Korma

This recipe was written down by Colonel Kenny-Herbert in the late-nineteenth century in his book *Culinary Jottings for Madras* (1885). This 'quoorma', as he spelt it, is a reminder that curry at that time was not always a mixture of cold meat re-hashed with a stock curry powder. I make no apology for lifting his recipe almost exactly as he detailed it because it is excellent, but I have halved the quantity of butter – the 4oz (115g) originally suggested seemed a little too much.

serves 4–6

about 700g (1lb 9oz) leg of lamb, fillet end for preference
55g (2oz) fresh root ginger, peeled and grated
1 teaspoon salt
55g (2oz) butter
2 medium onions, sliced
2 garlic cloves, finely chopped
spice mixture: made from 1 teaspoon coriander seed, 1 teaspoon black peppercorns, ½ teaspoon cloves and ½ teaspoon cardamom seeds ground together
150ml (5fl oz) single cream
100g (3½oz) almonds, blanched
1 dessertspoon turmeric
1 teaspoon sugar
the juice of 2 limes

Cut the meat into neat pieces, about 2cm (¾in) square, discarding any bone and fat. Put the pieces in a bowl with the grated ginger and salt, then stir well and leave to marinate in a cool place for about 2 hours.

Melt the butter in a heavy flameproof casserole. Add the onions and garlic and cook gently until they begin to turn light gold – this will take about 30 minutes. Then add the meat mixture and fry, turning frequently, until well browned.

Stir in the spice mixture and cook gently for a few minutes. Warm the cream to almost boiling point and put it with the almonds in a blender. Blitz together to reduce the almonds to fragments, then press through a sieve; use a little water to help the process if the mixture is very thick. Stir the almond-flavoured cream into the meat along with the turmeric and sugar.

Place the casserole over the lowest possible heat and cook gently for 40 minutes. Stir frequently, making sure that it doesn't stick. Add a little water as necessary. Check to make sure the meat is cooked through, then stir in the lime juice.

Braised Lamb Shanks

Lamb shanks usually remained attached to roasts of lamb until the early 1980s, at which point a change in fashion liberated them to become foundations for dishes in their own right. Slowly cooked in rich, savoury sauces, they have become a modern British classic.

serves
4

4 lamb shanks
2 tablespoons olive oil, plus extra
    for frying
300ml (10fl oz) red wine
salt and black pepper
1 large onion, chopped finely
2 garlic cloves, chopped finely
the leaves from 1 sprig rosemary,
    chopped finely

1 generous tablespoon flour
bouquet garni of a few sprigs
    each of parsley, marjoram,
    mint and basil plus 2 strips
    of orange zest
about 150ml (5fl oz) lamb or
    beef stock

Put the lamb shanks in a suitable bowl and add the oil, wine, 1 teaspoon salt and some pepper. Cover and leave the meat in the marinade for at least 2 hours (overnight is better). Turn the meat in the mixture occasionally. When ready to cook, drain the meat from the marinade, reserving the marinade for the sauce.

Heat a little olive oil in a flameproof casserole. Add the onion, garlic and rosemary and fry briskly, stirring frequently, until it is just beginning to turn golden. Pat the meat dry, toss it in the flour and add to the mixture, turning well until lightly browned. Dust in any remaining flour. Pour in the marinade, stir well and bring to the boil, stirring well. Add the bouquet garni and the stock and return the mixture to the boil.

Cover the casserole with foil and then with the lid. Transfer to a preheated oven, 150°C (300°F, Gas mark 2), and cook for 2½–3 hours. At the end of cooking time, taste the sauce and add more seasoning if necessary.

Serve with mashed potato or baked jacket potatoes.

Lamb Stewed with Samphire, Capers & Artichokes

Recipes using flavours derived from maritime environments appear in cookery books from the seenteenth century onwards. Here is one inspired by dishes mentioned by Jos Cooper in *The Art of Cookery Refin'd and Augmented* (1654) and Robert May in *The Accomplisht Cook* (1685). Use mutton if it is available: this was a dish for meat with depth of flavour. Samphire is a plant with fleshy, brilliant green stems. It grows on salt marshes, which are often used for grazing sheep, and is available from fishmongers from late May until September. It is a winter food and habitat for certain birds, so always check that it is sustainably harvested.

Fresh artichokes can be used if available: buy four, trim away the tops of the leaves, remove the thistly choke from the centre and boil for a few minutes until tender, then add them to the stew.

serves 4

2 tablespoons olive oil
1 small onion, finely chopped
1 garlic clove, crushed
about 750g (1lb 10oz) lamb or
    mutton chops, loin, chump
    or best end of neck
1 tablespoon flour
100ml (3½fl oz) red wine
1 anchovy, either salted or preserved in oil

150ml (5fl oz) beef stock or water
a little nutmeg
100g (3½oz) samphire
25g (1oz) salted capers
100–125g (3½–4½oz) globe artichokes
    preserved in oil (drained weight)
salt and black pepper
chopped parsley, to serve

Heat 1 tablespoon olive oil in a frying pan or flameproof casserole and add the onion and garlic. Cook gently, stirring frequently, until soft and golden. Remove with a slotted spoon and set aside.

Trim any excess fat off the chops, then coat lightly with flour. Add the remaining olive oil to the pan and fry them on both sides until lightly browned. Sprinkle in any remaining flour and stir well. Still stirring, add the wine and bring to the boil, then add the anchovy and stock or water. Mix well and bring to a simmer. Grate in a little nutmeg and add a couple of turns of black pepper. Cover and simmer very gently or put the casserole in a preheated moderate oven, 180°C (350°F, Gas mark 4), for about 45 minutes, or until the meat is tender.

Rinse the samphire and pick it over, discarding any soft or discoloured bits. Rinse the capers free from salt, and drain any oil from the artichokes. Cut these into quarters if this has not already been done.

When the meat is cooked, skim off any excess fat. Add the samphire, capers and artichokes to the stew, stir gently, and return to the oven for 5–10 minutes, just long enough for the samphire to cook and the capers and artichokes to heat through. Taste and add salt if necessary, but this is unlikely because the capers and anchovy will provide plenty.

Dust the stew with chopped parsley and serve hot with new potatoes.

Lamb's Liver with Orange

Liver gained a bad reputation in British cookery, probably through school meals when it was served cooked to a texture like shoe leather. However, if it is stewed gently with plenty of seasonings until just cooked, it is very different.

serves
4

about 25g (1oz) fat (lard
   or beef dripping)
1 large onion, thinly sliced
1 garlic clove, crushed
400g (14oz) lamb's liver,
   cut into thin slices
20g (¾oz) flour

zest of ½ orange, finely grated; and
   the juice of the whole orange
about 150ml (5fl oz) strong
   beef stock
pinch of chilli powder
salt and black pepper

Melt the fat in a frying pan. Fry the onion and garlic gently until translucent, then remove them with a slotted spoon and put on one side. Dust the liver with flour and fry lightly on both sides. Stir any remaining flour into the fat, then return the onion to the pan. Stir in the orange zest and juice, the beef stock, a small pinch of chilli powder, 1 scant teaspoon salt and a generous grinding of black pepper. Stir well, then cover and cook over a low heat.

Test after 5 minutes by inserting the end of a sharp knife into one of the liver slices – if the juices run very red, cook for another 5–10 minutes. It tastes best if the meat is just cooked. Taste and add more seasoning if desired.

Serve with a bowl of fluffy mashed potato.

Belly Pork Braised with Cider

Belly pork is usually cooked by roasting, but it is good rolled around a seasoning of herbs, braised gently and served cold – better than leaner cuts that tend to be dry. Choose the meat carefully, looking for a reasonable but not excessive layer of fat on top. Ask the butcher to remove the skin and bones, but take them home with you for the stock.

serves
6

about 1kg (2lb 4oz) piece of belly
   pork, skin and bones trimmed
   and reserved
generous pinch of chilli powder
1 teaspoon fennel seeds, bruised
2 tablespoons finely chopped parsley
leaves from 6–8 sprigs thyme

2 garlic cloves, cut into slivers
grated zest of 1 lemon
15g (½oz) lard
200ml (7fl oz) cider
200ml (7fl oz) stock (preferably
   beef)
salt and black pepper

Put the pork, fat-side down, on a board. Sprinkle with salt and grind a generous quantity of black pepper over it. Scatter with the chilli powder, fennel seeds, parsley, thyme, garlic and lemon zest. Roll up and tie firmly with kitchen string. The pork can be left overnight if desired.

When ready to cook, heat the lard in a flameproof casserole that will hold the meat neatly. Brown on all sides, then pour in the cider and let it bubble. Add the stock and bring to a gentle simmer. Tuck the skin and bones down beside the meat. Cover and transfer to a moderate preheated oven, 160°C (325°F, Gas mark 3), for 2½–3 hours, by which time the pork should be very tender.

Remove the pork from the cooking liquor and allow it to cool a little. Wrap in greaseproof paper, put between two boards and press lightly – a 900g (2lb) weight or a couple of cans of tomatoes on top are adequate. Leave until cold. Taste the cooking liquor and season if necessary. Strain into a bowl and chill, then remove any fat from the top. The stock should set to a jelly.

To serve, cut the pork into very thin slices. Chop the jelly and use it as a garnish. Serve with a salad of mixed leaves tossed in a mustardy dressing.

Normandy Pork Stew

This is a variation on the idea of the Harrico of Mutton (see page 31). The original recipe was given by Eliza Acton (1845). Loin chops work well with the new potatoes in this recipe.

serves
4

500–600g (1lb 2oz–1lb 5oz) pork chops from the loin or spare rib
1 tablespoon flour
20g (¾oz) butter or oil, such as sunflower
300–400ml (10–14fl oz) light pork or chicken stock

4 spring onions, trimmed and tied in a bunch with some parsley stems
500–600g (1lb 2oz–1lb 5oz) small new potatoes, scrubbed or scraped as preferred
salt and black pepper
chopped parsley, to garnish

Trim the chops of any excess fat. Mix the flour, 1 teaspoon salt and some pepper, and dust the chops with it. Heat the butter or oil in a large frying pan and brown the chops on both sides.

Sprinkle in any leftover flour and stir to amalgamate with the fat. Stir in the stock and bring to the boil. Add the spring onions and the parsley stems. Cover the pan, reduce the heat and allow the stew to simmer very gently for 30–45 minutes. At the end of this time, add the potatoes in a single layer on top of the meat. Cover and cook for about 30 minutes, or until the potatoes are tender.

Remove the pan from the heat, then fish out the bunch of parsley stems and spring onions and discard them. Allow to settle for a few minutes, then skim off any excess fat. Check the seasoning and adjust if necessary. Scatter a little chopped parsley over each portion and serve.

Faggots

Faggots are little bundles of pork meat and offal, wrapped in caul fat (a transparent membrane laced with fat, which lines the abdominal cavity of pigs and other meat animals). They belong to the now-extinct rural tradition of pig killing, and in the first half of the twentieth century became the food only of the poor. Recipes for them underwent a certain amount of innovation when the idea of the gastropub first evolved in the late 1990s. This is my own updated version.

serves
4–6

200g (7oz) boneless pork, such as loin steaks – try to buy some with a reasonable amount of fat, about 25 per cent of the total
200g (7oz) pork liver
200g (7oz) stewing veal
100g (3½oz) bacon, rinds removed
1 generous tablespoon chopped parsley
1 generous teaspoon chopped marjoram
1 generous teaspoon thyme leaves (lemon thyme if possible)

2 large garlic cloves, crushed
100g (3½oz) shallots, finely chopped
1 teaspoon salt
2 tablespoons brandy
finely grated zest of 1 lemon
a piece of caul fat from a pig
300ml (10fl oz) strong stock from pork, chicken or beef
ground black pepper

Mince the pork, liver, veal and bacon together and put in a bowl. Add all the other ingredients except the caul fat and stock. Season with ground black pepper. Mix with your hands to make sure everything is evenly distributed. Divide the mixture into 18–20 equal pieces and form into balls.

Put the caul fat in a bowl of tepid water for a few minutes. Carefully unravel it to give a large sheet. Use kitchen scissors to cut it into small pieces, about 8cm (3¼in) square, avoiding any bits that are very fatty. Drain the pieces and wrap each ball of faggot mixture in one, trimming any excess caul.

Put the faggots in a baking dish that holds them neatly. Pour the stock around them, and bake in a preheated moderate oven, 180°C (350°F, Gas mark 4), for about 1 hour. They should be cooked through and the tops nicely browned. At the end of the cooking time, pour off the cooking juices (keep the faggots warm in a low oven), allow the fat to rise and skim off as much as possible. Then reheat to boiling, pour back around the faggots and serve.

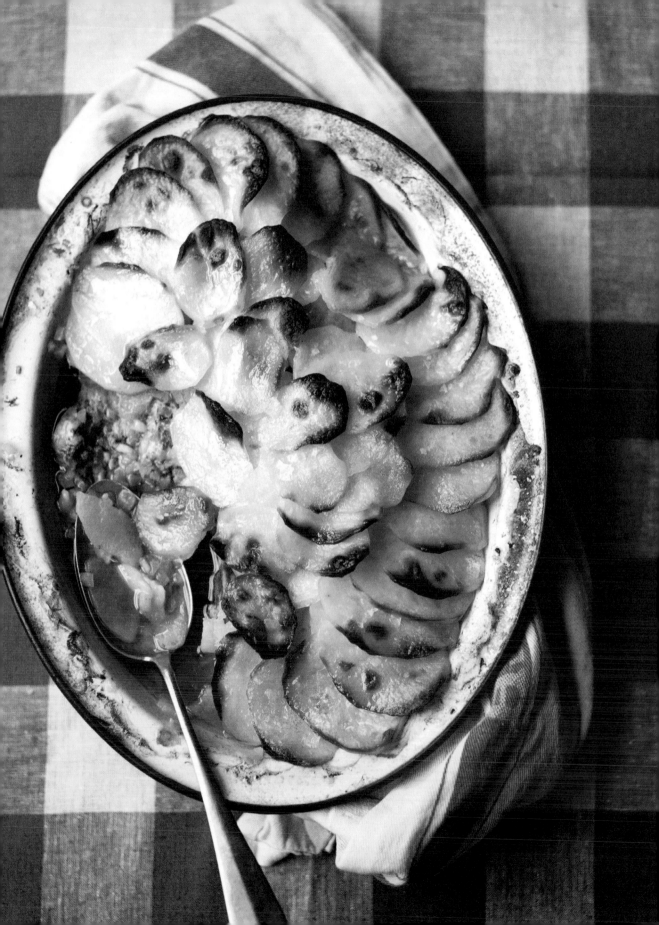

Pork with Potatoes & Apples

This is really a pork version of a hotpot. Verjuice is the juice of unripe grapes and is available bottled from some delicatessens. It has a subtle sour-sweetness, good with all sorts of rich meat. If it is unavailable, a mixture of white wine and lemon juice in the proportions of about 3:1 is the best substitute. Use a potato peeler to peel off the lemon zest.

serves
4

4 spare rib pork chops, total weight
    about 800g (1lb 12oz)
1 medium onion, peeled
2 garlic cloves, peeled
8 juniper berries
a strip of lemon zest

2 eating apples (Cox or russet for
    preference)
125ml (4fl oz) verjuice
800g–1kg (1lb 12oz–2lb 4oz) potatoes
about 20g (¾oz) butter
salt

Put the meat in a deep ovenproof pie dish or casserole. Chop the onion, garlic, juniper berries and lemon zest together until quite fine. Mix with the pork, add salt, then cover and leave to marinate for 2 hours.

Peel and core the apples, then cut them into thin slices. Layer over the pork. Pour in the verjuice. Then peel the potatoes and slice them thinly as well. Use them to cover the pork and apples, sprinkling lightly with salt and dotting with butter as you go. Cover the top with buttered greaseproof paper or foil.

Cook in a preheated low oven, 140°C (275°F, Gas mark 1), for 2 hours. At the end of this time, turn the heat up to 200°C (400°F, Gas mark 6), remove the cover and allow the top layer of potatoes to brown and crisp.

Pork with Apple Juice & Quinces

Pork and apples go well together, whether it's because the pigs have been feeding on windfalls in an orchard or the meat has been cooked with apples or their products. This recipe uses apple juice but replaces the more usual sliced apples in the sauce with quinces – a related species, but with a distinctive perfumed aroma. Use a potato peeler to peel off the lemon zest.

serves
4

25g (1oz) butter
4 pork spare rib steaks, total weight
    about 800g (1lb 12oz)
2cm (¾in) length of cinnamon stick,
    ground
8 cloves, ground
1 teaspoon peppercorns, ground
a thumb-sized piece of fresh root
    ginger, peeled and cut into thin
    matchsticks

3–4 strips lemon zest
350ml (12fl oz) apple juice
1 dessertspoon soft brown sugar
1 large or 2 small quinces, cut into
    quarters, the pips and core removed
about 1 teaspoon salt

Melt the butter in a flameproof casserole and brown the pork steaks on both sides. Remove them and keep to one side. Add the ground spices, ginger and the strips of lemon zest to the residual butter and cook gently, stirring all the time, for 3–4 minutes. Then pour in the apple juice, bring to the boil and cook until the liquid has reduced by about one-third.

Stir in the sugar, then add the pork steaks, quinces and salt. Seal, covering the dish with foil and the lid, if it has one. Cook in a preheated oven, 140°C (275°F, Gas mark 1), for about 2 hours, or until the pork is tender.

Serve with a mixture of potatoes and parsnips mashed together.

Pork Meatballs with Saffron Sauce

This recipe was inspired by a dish of small pear-shaped meatballs, which appears in several cookery books of the late seventeenth and early eighteenth centuries. The original was based on veal, but the recipe works well with pork, too. The egg yolk and lemon juice thickening gives the sauce a pleasing acid note, which is good with the rich meat.

serves
4

400g (14oz) minced pork
55g (2oz) fresh white breadcrumbs
leaves from 3–4 sprigs thyme
1 generous tablespoon finely
    chopped parsley
grated zest of 1 lemon, and the juice
    of ½ lemon

about ¼ teaspoon ground cloves
2 eggs, separated
pinch of saffron threads
300ml (10fl oz) stock, pork
    or chicken for preference
sage leaves and stems, to serve
salt and black pepper

Put the pork, breadcrumbs, thyme, parsley, lemon zest, cloves, 1 scant teaspoon salt and some pepper in a large bowl. Add the egg whites. Mix well and divide into 16 portions. For an authentically seventeenth-century look, roll into pear shapes, wider at one end than the other.

Heat a deep frying pan or a flameproof casserole. Add the saffron strands and let them toast gently for a moment – only enough to release their fragrance; don't let them burn. Pour in the stock and bring to the boil. Add the meatballs and simmer gently, turning two or three times, for 30–45 minutes.

Just before serving, beat the egg yolks with the lemon juice. Remove the meatballs to a warm serving dish. Off the heat, pour the egg and lemon mixture into the sauce. Heat very gently, stirring all the time, until the sauce has thickened a little and is thoroughly hot. Taste, correct the seasoning and pour around the meatballs. Garnish each 'pear' with a sage leaf and stem.

Serve immediately in the sauce with plain boiled rice.

Sausage & Lentil Stew

The fresh sausages of British tradition often lack the robustness and seasoning power of their European cousins but are still good with lentils, echoing the long-time combination of pork with pulses. A well-made Cumberland sausage, meaty and highly peppered, is good for this recipe. If it has been made properly, it should arrive coiled up in a long piece rather than formed into links. Cut into suitable lengths before cooking.

serves
4

1 tablespoon lard, goose fat or olive oil
1 medium onion, finely chopped
leaves from 3–4 sprigs rosemary,
    chopped
4 garlic cloves, chopped
600–700g (1lb 5oz–1lb 9oz)
    good-quality pork sausages

200ml (7fl oz) red wine
300g (11oz) small green lentils
    or Puy lentils
400ml (14fl oz) water
1 tablespoon Dijon mustard
salt and black pepper

Heat the fat or oil in a heavy frying pan or flameproof casserole. Add the onion, rosemary and garlic and cook briskly, turning frequently, until the onion begins to brown in patches. Add the sausages and allow to cook gently, turning every so often, so that they brown a little.

Pour in the wine and let it bubble a little, then add the lentils, water and some black pepper. Bring to the boil, transfer to a casserole dish, cover and put into a preheated oven, 160°C (325°F, Gas mark 3).

Cook for about 30 minutes and then check the stew. If the lentils seem to be drying out, add a little more water, preferably boiling. Return to the oven for another 20–30 minutes, after which the lentils should be soft but still holding their shape. Mix the mustard into the casserole, then taste and check the seasoning – the sausages will probably have made the mixture salty enough, but add a little more as necessary.

Serve with a salad of watercress or other sharp leaves, and some good bread.

Chicken in Red Wine

This recipe, based on the French *coq au vin*, is reminiscent of rich, meaty eighteenth-century ragoos and chickens cooked *à la braise*. True *coq au vin* is difficult to make properly without the vital ingredient – a cockerel weighing in at several kilos, with richly flavoured dense meat that needs slow cooking. However, a good free-range chicken and careful preparation and seasoning will give a delicious stew, which is well worth the effort.

serves 4–6

150g (5½oz) fat bacon or pancetta, diced
about 16 small shallots or button onions, peeled
250g (9oz) mushrooms (small open ones with dark gills are best)
about 20g (¾oz) butter
a chicken weighing about 2kg (4lb 8oz), cut into 8 joints
1 medium onion, chopped

1 medium carrot, chopped
4 garlic cloves, crushed
100ml (3½fl oz) brandy
1 bottle red wine (Burgundy for preference)
1 bay leaf
3–4 sprigs thyme
1 teaspoon concentrated beef stock
salt and black pepper

Fry the bacon or pancetta until crisp andmost of the fat has been given up. Remove and set aside. Add the button onions to the pan and fry until they colour a little. Add them to the bacon. Fry the mushrooms until the tops turn golden and add them to the bacon and onions. Add the butter to the remaining bacon fat and fry the chicken, skin-side down, until golden. Put these to one side. Add the onion, carrot and garlic to the pan and cook briskly, stirring frequently, until the onion softens. Warm the brandy in a ladle, ignite it and pour it into the pan, stirring well. When the flames die down, add the wine, bay leaf, thyme and concentrated stock. Bring to the boil and cook rapidly until reduced by half.

Remove the herbs, cool a little and blitz in a blender or food processor. Transfer to a casserole. Add the chicken, mushrooms, onion, bacon and seasoning. Cook in a preheated oven, 180°C (350°F, Gas mark 4), for 40 minutes, stirring halfway through. Check that the thickest parts of the chicken joints are fully cooked (if they are still a little pink, cook for a few more minutes). Season to taste. A bowl of pasta, with a knob of butter and a tablespoon of finely chopped parsley stirred through, makes a good accompaniment to this dish.

Fricassée of Chicken & Asparagus

1 chicken weighing about 1.5kg
    (3lb 4oz)
grated zest and juice of 1 lemon
leaves of 4–6 large sprigs fresh thyme
1 tablespoon chopped parsley
25g (1oz) butter
1 small onion, finely chopped
1 generous tablespoon flour

250ml (9fl oz) good chicken stock
2 bunches asparagus, washed, the
    woody ends of the stems discarded
    and the rest cut into pieces about
    2cm (¾in) long
75ml (2½fl oz) single cream
salt and black pepper

Cut the legs away from the body of the chicken and divide them into thighs and drumsticks. Cut the breasts and wings off the bird. Divide each in two, leaving a portion of breast meat attached to each wing. Trim the tips off the wings. Skin the joints, putting the skin and carcass in the stockpot.

Mix together the lemon zest and juice, thyme and parsley. Grind in a generous amount of black pepper. Put the chicken joints into this mixture, turning them to coat well, then cover and leave to marinate for at least 2 hours (overnight if possible). Stir the meat around in the marinade from time to time.

To start the fricassée off, melt the butter in a frying pan and cook the onion gently until translucent. Lift it out and put it into a flameproof casserole or large pan. Remove the chicken from the marinade (reserve any remaining juices). Dust the joints with flour and brown them lightly in the butter used for frying the onions. Add them to the casserole or pan. Add any remaining flour to the frying pan, stir well to mop up any fat, and add two-thirds of the stock and any leftover marinade. Stir well, scraping up any residues from frying, and bring to the boil. Season with ½ teaspoon salt and pour over the chicken. Cover, and simmer over a very low heat for about 1 hour, or until the chicken pieces are cooked through. If it seems to be drying up, add a little more stock, but don't overdo it.

Cool a little and skim off any excess fat. Add the asparagus and return to the heat for 5–10 minutes, until the asparagus is just cooked. Add the cream, stir gently and heat through. Taste, adjust the seasoning and serve with new potatoes or rice.

Chicken & Tomato Stew

This recipe is derived from a stew my mother sometimes made. She used it for cooking the hens from her poultry flock that had passed their prime, becoming what she called 'boiling fowl'. They were not as tender as chickens but had lots of flavour.

serves 4–6

55g (2oz) butter or 4–5 tablespoons
    sunflower oil
1 large onion, finely chopped
2–3 garlic cloves, crushed
leaves from 1 sprig rosemary,
    chopped
25g (1oz) flour

1 large chicken, preferably
    free-range, about 2kg
    (4lb 8oz), skinned and
    jointed into 10–12 pieces
250ml (9fl oz) white wine
6–8 plum tomatoes, or
    400g (14oz) canned tomatoes
salt and black pepper

Heat the butter or oil in a large frying pan. Add the onion, garlic and rosemary, and fry briskly, stirring frequently, until the onion begins to form pale golden patches. Use a slotted spoon to transfer it to a casserole.

Season the flour and use to dredge the chicken pieces, then fry gently until golden in the fat used for frying the onion. Add the chicken pieces to the casserole.

Sprinkle any remaining flour into the pan and stir well, then pour in the white wine and keep stirring, scraping any up residues from the base of the pan. When the mixture has come to the boil, add it to the casserole.

If using fresh tomatoes, cover with boiling water for 2 minutes, then drain them and peel off the skins. Cut each one in half, and add to the casserole. Canned tomatoes can be added as they are, straight from the can, including the juice.

Cover the casserole and cook in a preheated oven, 180°C (350°F, Gas mark 4), for about 1½ hours. Taste and correct the seasoning. Serve with steamed or mashed potatoes, or plain boiled rice.

Chicken Curry

1 chicken or chicken portions, about
   1.5–2kg (3lb 4oz–4lb 8oz)

3 small onions, sliced (add the onion
   skin and trimmings to the stock)

1 carrot, trimmed and peeled

1 celery stalk

a few black peppercorns

2 garlic cloves, peeled

1 dessertspoon turmeric

1 dessertspoon grond coriander seeds

1 teaspoon cayenne pepper

1 teaspoon sugar

1 teaspoon salt

2cm (¾in) cube of fresh root
   ginger, peeled

juice of 1 lime

55g (2oz) butter

about 1 tablespoon flour

1 heaped tablespoon curry powder

1 teaspoon ground cinnamon

150ml (5fl oz) coconut milk

1 bay leaf

1 tablespoon mango chutney

sprigs fresh coriander, to garnish

Joint the chicken and remove the skin. Cover the meat and refrigerate. Put the
skin and chicken carcass in a stockpot with the onion skins, carrot, celery and
black peppercorns, cover with water and simmer to make stock.

While this is cooking, make a seasoning paste: take one of the onions, one garlic
clove, the turmeric, coriander, cayenne, sugar, salt and ginger and process them
together in a blender. Add a little of the lime juice if it seems dry.

Melt the butter in a large pan. Dust the chicken pieces lightly with flour and fry
until golden. Drain and set aside. Add the sliced onions and remaining garlic clove
(crushed) and fry briskly. Stir frequently and cook until golden. Stir in the curry
powder and cook for 1 minute, then add the seasoning paste and cinnamon.
Fry gently for a few minutes before stirring in 150ml (5fl oz) chicken stock and
100ml (3½fl oz) coconut milk. Simmer for 15 minutes. Next add the bay leaf,
the chutney and the remaining lime juice. Add the chicken pieces, bring to the boil
and simmer very gently until the chicken is tender and cooked through – about
45 minutes, depending on the size of the pieces. Stir occasionally and add a little
more stock if it shows signs of drying out.

Once the chicken is cooked, stir in the remaining coconut milk. Taste and adjust
the seasoning. Garnish with coriander leaves and serve with plain boiled rice.

Chicken with Prunes & Saffron Broth

This simple but well-flavoured light stew is based loosely on the Scottish cock-a-leekie, which involves a chicken and a piece of beef cooked in broth with prunes and leeks. I've omitted the beef and leeks from this recipe. Use a good-quality chicken; this can be cooked whole in the broth and carved afterwards if desired, but it is easier to handle if cut into joints.

serves
4

12 ready-to-eat prunes
2 tablespoons whisky (optional)
400ml (14fl oz) strong chicken stock
12 whole peppercorns
a pinch of saffron threads

1 sprig parsley
1 chicken, about 1.5–2kg
    (3lb 4oz–4lb 8oz), cut into 4 joints
salt

The evening before you want to make the stew, put the prunes in a small bowl with the whisky and stir them around in it. If you don't want to use whisky, omit this step and proceed as below.

When ready to cook, pour the stock into a large pan and add the prunes plus any whisky they haven't soaked up, the peppercorns, saffron and sprig of parsley. Bring to a simmer, add the chicken pieces, season with 1 scant teaspoon salt and cover. Simmer gently for 30–40 minutes, or until the chicken pieces are cooked all the way through.

Serve each chicken joint in a deep plate, adding a generous amount of broth and two or three prunes to each helping. Boiled floury potatoes or potatoes mashed with cooked leeks are good accompaniments to the stew.

Braised Turkey & Celery with Tarragon Dumplings

The combination of turkey and celery is a neglected classic of the English kitchen. Maybe this is because nineteenth-century versions requiring a whole boiled turkey and a sauce based on several heads of celery look daunting, but the combination works well in a less grand manner.

serves
4

20g (¾oz) butter
4 small shallots, finely chopped
400–500g (14oz–1lb 2oz) turkey
    thigh, diced
20g (¾oz) flour
2–3 sprigs lemon thyme
grated zest of ½ lemon
about ½ teaspoon ground mace
400ml (14fl oz) strong turkey or
    chicken stock
salt and black pepper

½ head celery, trimmed and cut into
    2cm (¾in) lengths

for the dumplings
115g (4oz) plain flour, plus a little
    for dusting
85g (3oz) white breadcrumbs
1 teaspoon baking powder
a generous pinch of salt
100g (3½oz) suet
1 tablespoon chopped tarragon
about 200ml (7fl oz) water

Melt the butter in a heavy frying pan. Add the shallots and cook gently for about 10 minutes, or until translucent. Toss the turkey meat in flour and fry until the outside is lightly coloured. Add the thyme, lemon zest and mace, then stir in the stock. Season with 1 scant teaspoon salt and a little pepper and add the celery. Bring to a simmer, transfer to a casserole dish and cover with a lid. Cook in a preheated oven, 160°C (325°F, Gas mark 3), for about 1 hour.

Meanwhile, make the dumpling mixture: put everything except the water in a bowl and mix well. Add the water gradually, stirring until it forms a soft, slightly sticky dough (add a little more water if necessary). Dust a board and your fingers with flour and form the dough into about 18–20 dumplings.

By now, the meat should be just cooked but not yet tender. Skim off any excess fat, taste and season. Put the dumplings on the stew and return to the oven, uncovered, for another 20–30 minutes, or until they are crisp on top and golden.

Daube of Turkey

Daube is a word now applied to a dish of meat and vegetables braised slowly. This old-fashioned dish of French farmhouse cookery uses specially shaped pots, which are bulbous with narrow necks. They hold the ingredients in layers and the small opening cuts down on evaporation. However, any deep pot will do. Ask the butcher for a piece of pork rind – this adds body and richness to the sauce. Chorizo is not traditional but goes well with turkey.

serves
4

turkey breast steaks, weighing about
    100–125g (3½–4½oz) each
a thin rasher of bacon for each steak
100g (3½oz) pork rind, cut in
    small pieces
1 medium onion, finely chopped
4–6 small shallots, finely chopped
1 medium carrot, cut in small dice
1 beef tomato, skin and seeds
    removed, flesh diced

1 clove garlic, crushed
100g (3½oz) chorizo sausage, cut
    in thick slices
bouquet garni of a piece of leek,
    celery stalk, 1 bay leaf, a few
    sprigs thyme and parsley and
    a strip of orange zest
400ml (14fl oz) white wine
salt and black pepper

Wrap each piece of turkey in a rasher of bacon. Blanch the pork rind by putting it in a small pan, adding boiling water and cooking for 2–3 minutes. Drain it. Mix the onion, shallots, carrot, tomato and garlic together.

Put the pork rind into an ovenproof pot and add a layer of vegetables. Put the chorizo sausage on top and scatter more vegetables over. Put the bacon-wrapped turkey steaks on top of this and add the bouquet garni. Season with some pepper and about ½ teaspoon salt (the sausage and bacon will also be salty, so be cautious). Cover with the remaining vegetables and pour in the wine.

Put the lid on the pot with a layer of foil underneath to make it airtight. Transfer to a preheated low oven, 140°C (275°F, Gas mark 1), for 2½–3 hours.

This daube can be eaten hot or allowed to cool in the pot for gentle re-heating. If the sauce seems thin, pour some into a small pan and reduce by fast boiling before returning it to the stew.

Stewed Duck with Green Peas

Recorded from the early eighteenth century onwards, stewed duck and green peas became a classic of English summer food. Success depends on good stock, which must be well flavoured. If in doubt about this, start with about half as much again, add a little onion, carrot, parsley and some mushroom trimmings and allow it to reduce gently to the amount required. Beef stock or gravy was always specified for this dish.

serves
4

25g (1oz) butter
1 duck, jointed, or 4 duck joints
flour, for dusting
100g (3½oz) pancetta or bacon,
    cut into matchsticks
8 small shallots, peeled and halved
2 tablespoons brandy
bouquet garni of parsley, thyme,
    1 bay leaf and 1 sprig mint
zest of ½ lemon, cut into thin strips
3–4 cloves, pounded to a powder
pinch of cayenne

350ml (12fl oz) well-flavoured
    beef stock
200g (7oz) frozen peas
4–6 spring onions, trimmed
    and finely sliced
leaves from 6–8 sprigs mint, finely
    chopped – about 1 generous
    tablespoon
leaves from 6–8 sprigs basil,
    torn into shreds
salt

Melt the butter in a wide pan. Dust the duck with flour, then brown slowly on both sides in the butter. Remove from the pan and pour off the fat.

Return the pan to a low heat. Spread the pancetta and the shallots over the base. Put the duck on top, then pour in the brandy and let it bubble. Add the bouquet garni, lemon zest, 1 scant teaspoon salt, cloves and cayenne. Pour in the stock, bring to a simmer and cover. Stew very gently for about 1 hour. Towards the end of this time, you can test the duck meat to see if it is cooked – the juices should run clear when you insert the point of a sharp knife. When done, transfer the pieces to a serving dish. Discard the bouquet garni. Skim off the excess fat.

Return the pan with the cooking juices to the heat. Add the peas and spring onions and bring to the boil. As soon as the peas are done, remove from the heat, stir in the mint and basil and serve with a bowl of little new potatoes.

Game Casserole

400–500g (14oz–1lb 2oz) meat cut
  from game birds and animals
  as available
2 tablespoons duck or goose fat,
  beef dripping or lard
1 medium onion, chopped
1 celery stalk, chopped
1 medium carrot, chopped
2 garlic cloves, peeled and crushed
1 teaspoon ground coriander

bouquet garni of 1 bay leaf, thyme,
  marjoram, parsley and a few strips
  of orange zest
200ml (7fl oz) red wine
10g (¼oz) dried porcini
200ml (7fl oz) boiling water
55g (2oz) bacon or pancetta, diced
1 tablespoon balsamic vinegar
  (optional)
salt and black pepper

Cut the meat as neatly as possible into 2cm (¾in) cubes. Heat the fat in a frying
pan and add the onion, celery and carrot. Fry briskly, turning often, until they
turn slightly golden. Add the garlic, coriander and bouquet garni and pour in the
wine. Simmer gently for 10–15 minutes, making sure that not too much liquid
evaporates. Pour everything into a large bowl and allow to cool, then add the
meat. Turn well in the mixture, cover and leave in a cold place overnight.

Next day, wash the porcini and put them in a small bowl. Pour over the boiling
water and leave for at least 30 minutes to infuse.

Tip the meat into a strainer over a bowl. Keep the marinade that drips through
and the bouquet garni. Heat a flameproof casserole and fry the bacon or pancetta
until it has yielded most of its fat. Remove the pieces and keep to one side. Blot
any excess liquid off the meat, then fry it in the bacon fat. When the pieces are
browned, remove from the pan. Pour in the reserved marinade and bring to the
boil, strain and return to the pan. Add the bouquet garni, the porcini and their
soaking liquid, all the meat, and salt and pepper to taste, then return to a simmer.

Cover with greaseproof paper or foil and then the lid of the casserole. Cook in
a preheated low oven, 150°C (300°F, Gas mark 2), for about 1½ hours, or until
the meat is cooked. Stir in the vinegar at the end, if using. This tastes good with
jacket potatoes and a dish of cabbage cooked with juniper berries.

Partridge with Juniper Berries

Juniper berries were apparently not much liked in eighteenth-century England, if Martha Bradley (1756) is to be believed; she comments on how strange their flavour was to palates that were unaccustomed to them, and recommends that they be soaked in boiling water before use, presumably to take away some of their bitterness. I've increased their impact by adding a little gin to the recipe as well. A small glass of white wine can be used instead if you prefer.

serves
4

4 partridges, trussed
    for roasting
4 rashers unsmoked bacon
20g (¾oz) butter
2 tablespoons gin
200ml (7fl oz) strong beef stock
8–10 juniper berries

a little lemon juice
10g (¼oz) butter kneaded with
    10g (¼oz) flour
lemon slices and bread croûtons,
    toasted in the oven, to garnish
salt

Cover the breasts of the birds with bacon and tie it on with thin string. Melt the butter in a flameproof casserole or small sauté pan. Brown the birds all over, then discard any fat from the pan. Warm the gin in a ladle, set light to it and pour it flaming over the birds. Add the beef stock and juniper berries, cover and simmer very gently for about 45 minutes. Turn the birds in the cooking liquid occasionally. At the end of the cooking time they should be just cooked through; test the thickest part of the legs and cook a little longer if necessary.

Remove the birds from the cooking liquid and keep warm. Strain the juices into a clean pan and add a squeeze of lemon juice. Taste and add salt if necessary. Distribute the butter and flour mixture over the surface of the liquid, shaking the pan, so it is absorbed. Heat gently until it just comes to the boil and the sauce thickens slightly. Pour round the birds and serve with lemon slices and croûtons.

Pheasant with Spiced Sausage & Peppers

This recipe is old-fashioned in the sense that it is based on one that was first published over 50 years ago by Elizabeth David in her book *French Provincial Cookery* (1960). This dish is very different to standard game recipes and well worth trying out.

serves 4–6

2 tablespoons butter, duck or goose fat
1 pheasant, jointed into 8 pieces
about 1 tablespoon flour, for dusting
125g (4½oz) unsmoked pancetta
   or bacon, in one piece
12 small shallots, peeled
4 garlic cloves, peeled
2 tablespoons brandy
1 fresh red chilli (optional), seeds
   removed, cut into fine slices or
   tiny dice

bouquet garni of several sprigs
   oregano, thyme, parsley and a
   couple of strips of orange zest
200g (7oz) Spanish chorizo sausage,
   cut into 1cm (½in) lengths
1 red pepper, seeds removed, cut into
   1cm (½in) dice
1 yellow pepper, seeds removed, cut
   into 1cm (½in) dice
200ml (7fl oz) game or chicken
   stock

Melt the butter or fat in a flameproof casserole. Pat the pheasant joints dry, then shake the flour over them. Brown them quickly in the fat and set aside.

Cut the pancetta or bacon into dice, about 1cm (½in) square, and add them to the fat. Cook fairly briskly, stirring from time to time, until the bacon fat is translucent. Add the shallots and continue cooking, stirring, so that they start to brown in places. Stir in the garlic cloves and cook a moment longer.

Warm the brandy in a ladle, let it catch light and pour over the bacon mixture. Shake the dish until the flames die down, then return the pheasant to the pan. Add the chilli, if using, and the bouquet garni. Put the chorizo on top, then the peppers. Pour in the stock. Cover tightly and simmer over very low heat for about 1 hour, or cook in a preheated oven, 160°C (325°F, Gas mark 3), for 1–1½ hours.

At the end of cooking time, uncover, stir well and taste. The bacon and sausage should have given enough salt to the sauce. Serve with plain boiled rice.

Haddock, Leek & Potato Stew with Mussels

This is recorded on the east side of the Atlantic, where lobscouse (traditional to the north-west coast of England and ports in Germany and Scandinavia) was sometimes made with salt fish. Onions were the usual vegetable, but leeks give a good flavour and pretty contrast of colour. Ask the fishmonger to skin the fish for you, but get him to put the skin in the parcel, together with some fish bones if possible.

serves 4

500–600g (1lb 2oz–1lb 5oz) haddock, skins and bones removed and reserved
a few stalks or leaves of parsley
1 celery stalk
2 leeks, washed, trimmed and cut into 2cm (¾in) slices (keep the trimmings)

about 600ml (1 pint) water
300g (11oz) mussels
2 large potatoes, cut into 1cm (½in) dice
50ml (2fl oz) single cream
a little fresh tarragon, chopped (optional)
salt and black pepper

Simmer the fish skin, bones, parsley, celery and leek trimmings in a pan with the water gently for 20 minutes, then strain, reserving the liquid as stock.

Pull the beards off the mussels, discarding any that don't close when tapped. Put them in a pan with a tight-fitting lid and steam over fairly high heat for a few minutes. Strain the liquor into the fish stock, and keep the mussels on one side.

Put the potatoes and sliced leeks in a pan or flameproof casserole. Pour over the stock and season with 1 scant teaspoon salt and a little pepper. Cook for about 10 minutes, until the potatoes are just tender. Cut the haddock into slices about 2cm (¾in) thick, and place on top of the vegetables. Simmer for 5 minutes, or until the fish is just done. Add the mussels and allow them to heat through.

Put the vegetables and fish into soup bowls and pour the cooking liquid over. Add a spoonful of cream to each portion and scatter with chopped tarragon.

Water Souchy

Water souchy is the anglicised name for *waterzooi*, a dish of Flemish cookery. It made several appearances in eighteenth-century English cookery books as a method for cooking freshwater fish, usually perch, simply boiled in water with a bunch of parsley. 'This seems a very insipid Dish in the Description, but there is something very pretty in the Taste of the small Fish this way,' wrote Martha Bradley in 1756. She used flounders. Like her, I use sea fish, and she is right about the fish needing to be relatively small. Later versions add wine and make a fish stock for the dish, an idea that I have followed here.

serves 4–6

1 kg (2lb 4oz) of white fish, mixed according to what is available – try haddock or cod, sea bass and lemon sole
1 small onion, sliced
1 small carrot, chopped
1 celery stalk, chopped
250ml (9fl oz) white wine
a small bunch of parsley

salt and black pepper

to serve
55g (2oz) butter, melted and mixed with 1 tablespoon chopped parsley
triangular croûtons of bread fried in butter

Remove any skin and bones from the fish, putting them in a stockpot and cutting the flesh into neat serving pieces. Keep this cool. Add the onion, carrot and celery to the fish skin and bones and cover with water. Bring to the boil and cook quickly for about 20 minutes to make a stock. Strain, discarding the debris.

Take a pan in which the fish pieces will fit in a single layer. Pour in the wine, bring to the boil and cook for a few minutes. Add the bunch of parsley and the pieces of fish and pour over the stock. It should just cover the fish – if it doesn't, add a little water. Season with 1 scant teaspoon salt and a little black pepper and bring to the boil. Simmer until the fish is just cooked; this will take about 7–10 minutes, depending on the thickness of the pieces.

Remove from the heat and divide the fish between soup bowls. Pour some of the cooking liquor over each portion. Put the parsley butter in a small bowl and serve this and the croûtons separately.

To Stew Soles

This recipe is based on one that appears in an early Scottish cookery book by Elizabeth Cleland: *A New and Easy Method of Cookery* (1755). A simple method for cooking soles or any other flat fish, it needs a wide shallow pan in which they will fit comfortably in a single layer. You can ask the fishmonger to remove the skins from the soles.

serves 2

2 small soles, each weighing about
    250g (9oz)
125ml (4fl oz) white wine
a few peppercorns
1 blade of mace
a strip of lemon zest, about
    3cm (1¼in) long
100g (3½oz) shelled prawns (optional)
1 generous teaspoon butter

1 generous teaspoon flour
salt

to serve
finely chopped parsley
lemon wedges
2–3 slices white bread, for making
    croûtons

Put the soles side by side in a shallow pan and pour the wine over them. Add the peppercorns, mace and lemon zest, and a good pinch of salt. Bring to a simmer, then cover (use foil if the pan doesn't have a lid) and cook over a low heat for 10 minutes. At the end of this time, the fish should be cooked through, although the upper side might not be quite done – the best way to deal with this is to put the pan under a hot grill for 2–3 minutes. Add a little water if the cooking liquid shows signs of evaporating – there should be about the same amount as at the start.

When the soles are cooked, remove them to warmed plates. Put the pan with the cooking liquid back over a low heat. Remove the spices and lemon zest and add the prawns, if using. Allow them to heat through to boiling. Knead the flour and butter together and dot over the surface of the liquid, shaking the pan so that it disperses and thickens the sauce. Stir and pour over the fish.

Sprinkle with parsley, and garnish with lemon wedges and toasted croûtons.

Cullen Skink

This is a version of a traditional Scottish soup of smoked fish and potatoes. I've altered it very slightly to push it closer to North American chowder-type dishes, and to create something in between a soup and a stew. It makes a good light lunch or supper dish.

serves
4

400–500g (14oz–1lb 2oz)
    smoked haddock
1 small onion, sliced
1 bay leaf
a few peppercorns

700g (1lb 9oz) floury potatoes, peeled
    and cut into 1cm (½in) cubes
100ml (3½fl oz) single cream
salt
snipped chives or 2 spring onions, very
    finely sliced, to garnish

Put the smoked haddock, sliced onion, bay leaf and peppercorns in a pan and cover with water. Heat and leave to simmer for about 10 minutes or until the fish is cooked. Remove it from the pan (keep the cooking liquid). When the fish has cooled enough to handle, remove all the skin and bones. Flake the flesh and set on one side. Return the bones and skin to the pan, cover and simmer for about 30 minutes longer to make a stock. Strain and measure it – you will need about 600–700ml (1–1¼ pints). If there isn't enough, make up the quantity with water.

Put the stock and the potatoes in a clean pan and bring to the boil. Let them simmer until the potatoes are well cooked and just starting to break up a little, giving body to the liquid. Stir in the fish and heat through. Taste and add more salt if desired; remember, the smoked fish may be quite salty. Stir in the cream.

Divide between four soup bowls and scatter each portion with snipped chives or a little spring onion. Serve piping hot with wholemeal bread.

Fricasséed Parsnips

Eighteenth-century cookery writers seemed to make everything into fricassées, including most vegetables. It is a good way of dealing with parsnips, whose texture and natural sweetness respond well to this treatment, as in a recipe based on one given by Hannah Glasse in 1747. You can eat this as a separate vegetable dish with some good crusty bread or use it as an accompaniment to plain grilled or roast beef or pork.

serves
4

600–700g (1lb 5oz–1lb 9oz) parsnips, peeled
100ml (3½fl oz) white wine
125ml (4fl oz) cream beaten with 2 egg yolks

15g (½oz) butter kneaded with 15g (½oz) flour
salt
pinch of nutmeg

Cut the parsnips into pieces, about 4cm (1½in) long, then cut these into wedges lengthways. Cook in boiling water until tender (about 10–15 minutes), then drain.

Wash the saucepan and add the wine. Bring it to the boil and add the parsnips. Cook gently for a moment, then remove the pan from the heat and pour in the cream-and-egg mixture. Heat very gently but don't allow it to boil. Dot the flour and butter over the top and continue to heat gently, shaking the pan until the mixture is absorbed into the sauce, which should thicken slightly. Season to taste with salt and a little nutmeg.

Peas with Cream

The idea of eating fresh green peas became fashionable sometime in the seventeenth century. They were often cooked with butter and herbs in the manner that we still know as *à la française*, but there were variations, such as adding cream. Serve this dish with good bread for a light lunch or supper, or to accompany egg or cheese dishes, or plainly grilled meat or fish.

serves
4

2–4 lettuce hearts, depending on size – use Little Gem, Cos or cabbage lettuces
20g (¾oz) butter
250g (9oz) green peas (shelled weight)
2 tablespoons water
½ teaspoon salt
½ teaspoon sugar

pinch of nutmeg
1 teaspoon butter kneaded with 1 teaspoon flour (optional)
4 tablespoons double cream
a mixture of fresh chives, mint, chervil or tarragon – enough to make about 2 tablespoons when finely chopped

Remove any raggedy outer leaves from the lettuces. Cut in half lengthways, wash them and then shake as dry as possible.

Put a frying pan over a very gentle heat and melt the butter. Add the lettuces, cut-side down. Put the peas in around them. Add the water, remembering that the lettuces will produce liquid as they cook. Sprinkle in the salt and sugar and grate in a little nutmeg.

Cover the pan closely (use foil if it doesn't have a lid) and cook, very gently, for 25 minutes. Check every few minutes at the start to make sure that it isn't drying up, and towards the end to see how much juice the vegetables have yielded. If there seems to be more than a couple of tablespoonfuls, remove the covering for the last few minutes.

At the end of the cooking time, remove the lettuce to a warmed serving dish (if there still seems to be a lot of juice in the pan with the peas, distribute the flour and butter mixture over the surface and heat gently, shaking the pan until the sauce thickens). Add the cream, stir well and heat until nearly boiling, then pour over the lettuce. Sprinkle with the chopped herbs and serve.

Sarah's Summer Vegetable Stew

This recipe, given to me by a friend, makes the most of late spring and summer vegetables. It is essentially an easy-going mixture of the best from the garden or the market. The onion, asparagus, broad beans and peas are essential; make up the remaining weight with a selection of the other vegetables listed. Sarah suggests crusty bread and pesto as accompaniments, but I add tiny butterballs and eat it with thin slices of French bread, dried in the oven until crisp.

serves
4

200g (7oz) asparagus
100g (3½oz) broad beans
   (after podding)
100g (3½oz) peas (after podding)
500g (1lb 2oz) other vegetables
   as available – choose from other
   bean varieties, such as French,
   runner or bobby beans; mangetouts
   or sugar peas; small courgettes;
   Florentine fennel; and young,
   small globe artichokes
150ml (5fl oz) olive oil
1 large onion, finely chopped
bouquet garni of 1 bay leaf, thyme and
   parsley, plus summer savory
   if available
300ml (10fl oz) white wine
salt

for the butterballs
60g (2¼oz) fresh breadcrumbs
25g (1oz) butter
1 egg yolk
pinch of salt
about 1 tablespoon chopped herbs
   to taste – a fines herbs mixture
   of parsley, chives, tarragon
   and chervil is good

Make sure all the vegetables are washed and prepared as appropriate. Discard any woody bits off the end of asparagus stems and cut the rest into 2cm (¾in) lengths. Trim beans, mangetouts or sugar peas and cut into 2cm (¾in) lengths as well. Trim courgettes and cut into short lengths if very small, or dice 1–2cm (½ –¾in) square if larger.

Trim fennel, discarding any tough or blemished outer layers and cut into dice like the courgettes. Trim the stems and cut the tops off globe artichokes, then scoop out and discard the thistle-like choke from the centre. Cut them in quarters.

Heat the oil in a large flameproof casserole. Add the onion, bouquet garni and the summer savory if available. Cook over a very low heat until the onions start to turn transparent. Then add the asparagus, broad beans, peas and whatever other vegetables have been chosen. Heat through, turning them all well in the oil. Add the white wine and 1 generous teaspoon salt. Bring to a simmer and cook gently, turning occasionally, until all the vegetables are cooked through but not too soft. Taste and check the seasoning.

Make the butterballs by whizzing the breadcrumbs, butter, egg yolk and salt in a blender. Stir in the chopped herbs and form into about 20 little balls the size of hazelnuts. Drop them into the cooked vegetable mixture and continue to simmer for 5 minutes.

Serve in deep bowls, adding pesto if you wish, and hand bread or toast separately.

Braised Celery

This vegetable dish has been in the English cookery repertoire for at least 200 years. It is a good side dish for roasts of game, especially venison, or can be served as a separate vegetable course with some crusty bread, in which case omit the croûtons.

serves
4

2 large heads celery
15g (½oz) butter
1 medium onion, finely chopped
1 small carrot, finely chopped
1 small slice of turnip, finely chopped
bouquet garni of 1 bay leaf, some
    thyme and parsley

about 500ml (18fl oz) strong beef
    stock
croûtons fried in butter, to garnish
salt

Trim the heads of celery, removing any particularly stringy outer stems. Cut in half lengthways, then wash well and blanch them quickly in a saucepan of boiling water. Cut in half crossways as well if the stems are very long.

Melt the butter in a pan that will hold the celery neatly in one layer. Add the onion, carrot and turnip, and cover the pan. Allow them to sweat gently for about 15 minutes, then put in the celery, cut-side down. Add the bouquet garni and pour over about two-thirds of the stock. Bring to a simmer and cook gently but steadily for about 2 hours. Add more stock as it evaporates, but towards the end of cooking allow it to reduce so that it becomes a fairly concentrated glaze.

Remove the celery and arrange it on a warmed serving dish. Taste the cooking liquid and add more seasoning if required. Strain it over the celery and garnish generously with the croûtons.

Butterbean Casserole

The idea of eating vegetable dishes that were actually vegetarian – no bits of bacon, no meat stock – was a novel one in late nineteenth-century Britain. The Food Reform Movement did their best within the conventions of the time, trying to work out substitutes for the vast amounts of protein seen as necessary for health. At the same time, things that would now be considered good additions, such as olive oil, garlic and herbs, weren't used either because of snobbish ideas about 'greasiness' and bad breath, or simply because they weren't obtainable. The butter bean stew made by my mother probably originated with ideas from this time and I have incorporated a few things either unavailable or frowned upon in earlier days.

serves
4

140g (5oz) dried butter beans
3–4 tablespoons olive oil
1 large onion, finely chopped
2 garlic cloves, finely chopped
leaves from 1 sprig rosemary,
    finely chopped
100ml (3½fl oz) white wine
bouquet garni of 1 bay leaf, a few
    sprigs parsley and some thyme
about 350ml (12fl oz) water
400ml (14fl oz) passata
    (sieved tomato pulp)
a handful of basil leaves, chopped

for the topping
4 slices good white bread, crusts
    removed, cut into triangles
about 4 tablespoons good olive oil
about 40g (1½oz) strongly flavoured
    cheese, such as Pecorino Romano
    or a good Cheddar, finely grated
1–2 tablespoons pine nuts (optional)
salt and pepper

Soak the beans overnight in cold water. The following day, bring them and the water to the boil and cook rapidly for 10 minutes. Drain, discarding the water.

Heat about 3 tablespoons olive oil in a flameproof casserole. Add the onion, garlic and rosemary. Cook briskly, stirring often, until the onion begins to brown slightly. Lower the heat and add the beans, turning them in the mixture.

Add the wine, bouquet garni and the water. Bring to the boil, cover the casserole and then cook either on a very low heat on the hob or in a preheated moderate oven, 150°C (300°F, Gas mark 2), for about 1¼ hours, or until the beans are soft. Stir occasionally and check the liquid level. Add a little more water if they seem to be drying out. When they are fully softened, season with about ½ teaspoon salt and some pepper. Turn the oven up to 200°C (400°F, Gas mark 6). Add the passata in a layer on top of the beans and scatter the chopped basil over the top.

Dip the pieces of bread in olive oil (lightly – don't try to saturate them) and arrange over the top as if making bread-and-butter pudding. Sprinkle with grated cheese and scatter over the pine nuts (if using). Return the dish to the oven, uncovered, and allow the topping to brown and crisp for about 10 minutes; check from time to time to make sure that it doesn't scorch.

This is a very filling dish and the best accompaniments are either a crisp salad or some lightly cooked summer vegetables.

Pies

Steak & Kidney Pie

Steak and kidney in puddings or pies had become a classic English combination by the early twentieth century. Nicely made and carefully seasoned, they remain one of the best dishes in our traditional repertoire. Earlier versions involved pieces of rump steak and kidney, uncooked, enclosed in suet crust and boiled as a pudding. Later ones evolved to be closer to a highly flavoured beef ragoo covered with puff pastry, as described here.

serves 4

40g (1½oz) dripping
1 large onion, chopped
40g (1½oz) flour, plus extra for dusting
500g (1lb 2oz) stewing beef, trimmed
    and cut into 2cm (¾in) cubes
140–200g (5–7oz) ox kidney, trimmed
    and cut into 1cm (½in) cubes

400ml (14fl oz) beef stock
1 bay leaf
½ teaspoon ground allspice
few drops of Worcestershire sauce
1 quantity puff pastry (see page 214)
beaten egg, cream or milk, to glaze
salt and black pepper

Melt a little of the dripping in a large frying pan and cook the onion gently for about 30 minutes until soft. Remove to a casserole.

Mix the flour with ½ teaspoon salt and some pepper. Toss the steak and kidney in this. Add the rest of the dripping to the frying pan and brown the meat, in batches if necessary, transferring to the casserole when done. Sprinkle any leftover flour into the frying pan to take up the remaining fat and gradually stir in the beef stock, scraping the base of the pan to incorporate all the juices from cooking the meat. Bring to the boil and cook for a few minutes, then pour it over the meat. Add the bay leaf, allspice and a shake of Worcestershire sauce.

Cover and cook in a preheated oven, 160°C (325°F, Gas mark 3), for about 2 hours. At the end, taste and add more seasoning as necessary.

Pour into a suitable pie dish and allow to cool. Dust a work surface with flour, roll out the pastry and cover the pie. Decorate with leaves made from the pastry trimmings, and then glaze with some beaten egg, cream or milk. Bake at 220°C (425°F, Gas mark 7) for 20 minutes to raise the pastry, then reduce the heat to 180°C (350°F, Gas mark 4) for a further 15–20 minutes, or until the filling is reheated thoroughly and piping hot.

Indian Shepherd's Pie

serves
4

3 tablespoons oil

3 cloves

3 cardamom pods

1 large onion, finely chopped

4 garlic cloves, crushed

2cm (¾in) cube of fresh root ginger,
    peeled and grated

1 teaspoon cumin seeds, toasted in a
    warm frying pan and then ground

1 teaspoon coriander seeds, ground

½ teaspoon turmeric

pinch of chilli powder, or to taste

450–500g (1lb–1lb 2oz) minced lamb

2 large tomatoes, peeled and chopped

100ml (3½fl oz) water

½–1 teaspoon garam masala

salt and black pepper

1 tablespoon chopped mint

for the topping

900g (2lb) potatoes, peeled
    and cut into chunks

100ml (3½fl oz) milk

40g (1½oz) butter

2 tablespoons chopped
    coriander leaves

1 fresh mild green chilli,
    finely chopped

chilli powder or hot fresh chilli
    (finely chopped), to taste

salt and black pepper

Heat the oil in a large frying pan. Add the cloves and cardamom and allow them to heat through, then add the onion. Fry gently, stirring frequently, until it is beginning to brown evenly – this will take at least 20 minutes.

Add the garlic and ginger and continue cooking for 1–2 minutes, then add the cumin, coriander and turmeric, plus a pinch of chilli powder. Stir well to heat the spices, then add the minced lamb. Keep stirring it and breaking up any lumps until the meat is lightly browned and the onion mixture is well amalgamated.

Add the tomatoes and the water, then turn the heat down low, cover the pan, and leave the mixture to simmer for a minimum of 1 hour, or 2 hours if possible. Stir from time to time and add a little water if it shows signs of drying out. At the end of the cooking time, stir in a little garam masala, salt to taste and the chopped mint. Pour the mixture into an ovenproof dish, then remove the cloves and the cardamom pods.

To make the topping, boil the potatoes, then drain and mash with the milk and butter, adding salt to taste and quite a lot of black pepper. Stir in the coriander leaves and the mild chilli; add a little chilli powder or hot chilli to taste.

Spread the mashed potato over the meat mixture, roughening the surface with a fork. Bake in a preheated oven, 190°C (375°F, Gas mark 5), for about 25–30 minutes, or until the potato is browning, or chill and reheat later, allowing about 40–45 minutes and making sure the pie is properly heated through.

Veal & Ham Pie

serves 4–6

400–500g (14oz–1lb 2oz) veal,
   preferably from the loin or leg
100–150g (3½–5oz) cooked ham in
   one piece
2 hard-boiled eggs
1 generous tablespoon chopped parsley
leaves from a few sprigs winter
   savory or thyme, chopped
15–20 large leaves of fresh basil,
   torn into pieces
2 bay leaves, spines removed and
   the leaves shredded
pinch cinnamon
125ml (4fl oz) well-reduced
   stock – veal for preference,
   otherwise chicken

salt and black pepper
1 quantity puff pastry (see page 214)
flour, for dusting
beaten egg, cream or milk,
   to glaze

for the forcemeat
200g (7oz) spinach, well washed
200g (7oz) breadcrumbs made
   with fresh white bread
55g (2oz) fat bacon (unsmoked),
   cut into small pieces
½ teaspoon salt
1 egg

Cut the veal, ham and hard-boiled eggs into thin slices. Mix together the parsley, winter savory or thyme leaves, half the basil leaves and the bay leaves. Add the cinnamon, salt and pepper. Toss the veal pieces in this and put on one side.

Put the spinach in a pan; the only water it will need is that left on the leaves from washing it. Put it over medium heat with a lid on. Stir until wilted, then tip it into a sieve and press well to remove excess water. Put it together with the breadcrumbs, bacon, remaining basil leaves and salt into a liquidiser or food processor, then blend to a paste. Add the egg and process just enough to mix.

Take a deep pie dish and put a layer of ham in the base. Cover this with some of the forcemeat. Add the slices of hard-boiled egg, then more forcemeat, then the veal, interspersed with any remaining forcemeat. Pour in the stock.

Roll out the pastry and cover the dish. Glaze with beaten egg, cream or milk. Cook in a preheated oven, 220°C (425°F, Gas mark 7), for 20 minutes, reduce to 180°C (350°F, Gas mark 4) and cook for a further 45 minutes to 1 hour.

Chicken & Wild Mushrooms in a Potato Case

The idea for this recipe came from another of Colonel Kenny-Herbert's recipes, in this case the suggestion of serving *chicken à la financière* in small drum-shaped cases made of deep-fried potato. Chicken cooked this way is, as the name suggests, a rich production and the original requires large quantities of truffles. Although still quite complex to make, this recipe is more modest. If the idea of the enclosing potato case is daunting, serve the stew separately, with the mash baked in a buttered dish and scattered with the crumbs and cheese as an accompaniment.

serves
4

1 chicken weighing about
    2–2.5kg (4lb 8oz–5lb 8oz)
1 carrot, trimmed and peeled
1 onion, peeled
1 celery stalk
bouquet garni of 1 bay leaf, some
    thyme sprigs and parsley stems
10g (¼oz) dried porcini mushrooms
25g (1oz) butter
55g (2oz) pancetta (unsmoked),
    cut into matchsticks
400g (14oz) mushrooms (about half
    ordinary button mushrooms and the
    rest, if possible, wild ones, such as
    chanterelles), washed and trimmed

25g (1oz) flour
100ml (3½fl oz) dry sherry
salt and black pepper

for the case
1.5kg (3lb 4oz) floury potatoes,
    peeled and cut into chunks
4 egg yolks
1 teaspoon salt
½ teaspoon mace
20g (¾oz) butter
20g (¾oz) breadcrumbs, made
    from stale bread
20g (¾oz) grated Parmesan

Joint the chicken and cut the meat from the breasts and thighs into neat cube, about 1.5cm (⅝in) square. Cover the meat and keep in the fridge. Put the bones and the skin in a large saucepan with the carrot, onion, celery and the bouquet garni. Cover with water, then bring to the boil and simmer gently for about 2 hours to make a good stock (use the wings and drumsticks for another dish, or add them to the stock pot).

Strain off the stock, skimming off as much fat as possible, then return 500ml (18fl oz) of it to a clean pan. Place this over a gentle heat and allow it to reduce to about one-third of the original volume. This will be needed for the stew.

When you're ready to make the stew, put the dried porcini mushrooms in a small bowl and add about 100ml (3½fl oz) boiling water. Then melt the butter in a frying pan and add the pancetta. Allow to cook gently until the fat is transparent. Remove and set aside. Slice the mushrooms and fry in the fat from cooking the bacon, cooking quite briskly and stirring frequently until they begin to brown. Drain and add to the pancetta.

Dust the chicken meat with flour and fry in the same pan, turning until lightly browned on all sides. Sprinkle in any remaining flour, stirring to absorb any fat in the pan, then add the sherry and let it bubble. Stir in the porcini and their soaking liquid, plus the fried mushrooms and pancetta. Add the reduced stock and mix well. Allow to cook very gently for about 30 minutes, by which time the chicken pieces should be well done. Taste and add salt and pepper as necessary.

For the potato case, boil the potatoes and mash (without additions). They are best passed through a ricer, a sieve or a mouli-legumes to make sure they are perfectly smooth. Beat in the egg yolks, salt and the mace, then return to the pan and stir them over a low heat for a few minutes to dry the mixture out a little.

Use some of the butter to coat the inside of a large pie dish. Use two-thirds of the potato mixture to line the base and sides, covering them as evenly as possible and making sure there are no gaps or thin patches through which the stew can escape. Carefully pour in the stew, ensuring that it doesn't come above the level of the potato lining. Dot the rest of the potato over the top, then use a fork to spread it evenly across to form a lid and seal the edges. Melt the remaining butter and stir into the breadcrumbs. Add the Parmesan and then sprinkle this mixture over the top of the potato.

Bake in a preheated oven, 200°C (400°F, Gas mark 6), for about 25 minutes, until the top is golden brown and the stew is thoroughly hot. Unmould the pie on to a deep dish if you feel brave; otherwise, serve from the cooking dish.

Chicken & Leek Pie

Chicken makes an excellent pie filling. In the time-honoured traditions of the English kitchen, it is often combined with ham, as is veal; mushrooms are another common addition. Leeks are less usual but they make a tasty filling for a winter pie.

serves
4

1 chicken
55g (2oz) flour, plus extra for dusting
scrape of nutmeg
55g (2oz) butter
a piece of lean ham or gammon,
 weighing about 200g (7oz),
 cut into 1cm (½in) cubes

4–6 leeks (depending on size), white
 part only, washed and cut into
 1cm (½in) lengths
300ml (10fl oz) chicken stock
1 quantity puff pastry (see page 214)
beaten egg, cream or milk, to glaze
salt and black pepper

Joint and skin the chicken as directed in Fricassée of Chicken and Asparagus (see pages 58–59). Season the flour with ½ teaspoon salt, some pepper and a good scrape of nutmeg. Dust the chicken joints with this mixture. Melt the butter in a large frying pan and brown the chicken lightly in it. Put the cubed ham or gammon into the base of a suitable pie dish. Put the chicken on top, and then add the sliced leeks.

Stir any remaining flour into the butter left in the pan, then stir in the chicken stock. Bring to the boil, stirring all the time, and cook for a few minutes. Taste to check the seasoning and add a little more if necessary. Pour this into the pie dish as well. Allow to cool a little.

Roll out the puff pastry on a lightly floured surface and then cover the pie. You can decorate it with pastry leaves, as taste and fancy suggest, and glaze with some beaten egg, cream or milk.

Bake in a preheated hot oven, 220°C (425°F, Gas mark 7), for 20 minutes to set the pastry, then reduce the heat to 180°C (350°F, Gas mark 4) and cook for a further 45–50 minutes until the pastry is golden and the filling cooked through.

Pigeon Pie

Pigeon pie is another dish that was once popular but now rarely makes an appearance on English tables. Early books contain numerous recipes for pigeons generally – the birds were easily accessible, kept in the dovecotes of large farms and manor houses. Nowadays we have to make do with leaner, smaller wood pigeons, but they still make good pies. In old recipes, pigeons were used whole, but I prefer to use only the breast meat.

serves
4

6–8 pigeons
55g (2oz) butter
250g (9oz) button mushrooms,
    trimmed and sliced
4–6 rashers of lean back bacon
    – about 150g (5oz)
250g (9oz) chicken livers
6–8 sprigs thyme, leaves only

2 tablespoons parsley, chopped
2 sprigs rosemary, leaves only
1 tablespoon snipped chives
55g (2oz) flour
1 quantity shortcrust pastry
    (see page 212)
beaten egg, for glazing
salt and black pepper

Put the pigeons in a pan into which they fit neatly, and cover with water. Bring them to the boil and simmer for about 30 minutes. Remove from the liquid and allow to cool a little. When you can handle them, cut the breasts off and any meat that can easily be taken from the legs. Put this on one side, return the bones to the liquid and continue to simmer to make a good game stock.

Melt the butter in a large pan and add the mushrooms. Cover and allow to cook until they have exuded quite a lot of liquid, then take the lid off the pan and continue to cook fast, stirring frequently, until most of this has evaporated.

Use the bacon to line a pie dish. Put the mushrooms on top. Examine the chicken livers to make sure the gall bladder (a small dark green sac) has been removed from them all, and cut each one into two to three pieces. Mix with the chopped herbs and distribute over the mushrooms. Then add the pigeon meat.

Put the pan in which the mushrooms were cooked back on the heat. Add the flour and stir well to make a *roux*. Cook gently to allow the flour to brown. Stir in enough reserved stock – about 500ml (18fl oz) – to make a fairly thick sauce and cook gently for a few minutes, stirring constantly. Season well, using about 1 teaspoon salt and plenty of pepper. Pour over the pigeon meat and allow to cool a little.

Roll out the pastry on a lightly floured surface and use to cover the pie. Crimp the edge and then cut a couple of holes in the middle for the steam to escape, and decorate with pastry leaves and flowers from the trimmings, as imagination suggests. Brush with beaten egg. Bake in a preheated hot oven, 200°C (400°F, Gas mark 6), for 20 minutes to set and glaze the pastry, then reduce the heat to 180°C (350°F, Gas mark 4) and cook for a further 45–50 minutes. The pie can be eaten hot but is best served cold (not chilled).

NOTE: If you have no objection to bones in your pie, halve the raw birds and omit the step of boiling them, remembering that their bones will not be available for making stock to go in the pie. Cook the pie for about 20 minutes longer.

Venison & Mushroom Pie

This recipe is adapted from the robust pub lunch tradition. The pie is more usually made with beef (which works equally well in this recipe), but it is a good way of using stewing venison.

serves
4

1 medium onion, peeled
60g (2¼oz) lard, beef dripping
   or light oil such as sunflower oil
2 garlic cloves, peeled
leaves from 2 sprigs rosemary
250g (9oz) button mushrooms,
   trimmed and sliced
500g (1lb 2oz) stewing venison,
   cubed

25g (1oz) flour, plus extra for dusting
150ml (5fl oz) red wine
about 300ml (10fl oz) game
   or beef stock
1 tablespoon chopped parsley
leaves from 4–5 sprigs thyme
1 quantity puff pastry (see page 214)
beaten egg, cream or milk, to glaze
salt and black pepper

Chop the onion fairly finely. Heat half the fat or oil in a large frying pan and add the onion. Let it cook quite briskly, stirring frequently. Chop the garlic and rosemary leaves small and add them to the onion. Keep frying and stirring until the onion is just beginning to go brown. Remove from the pan with a slotted spoon and put in a casserole dish.

Fry the mushrooms in the fat remaining in the pan. Keep the heat quite high, so that any juice they exude evaporates. When they have browned a little, add them to the onion mixture.

Toss the venison in some flour. Add the remainder of the fat to the frying pan, if necessary, and brown the venison in batches, transferring it to the casserole when done. Dust any remaining flour into the frying pan and stir to absorb any residual fat. Pour in the wine and keep stirring, scraping up the residues from the base of the pan. Add two-thirds of the stock and bring to the boil, stirring constantly. Add the chopped parsley, thyme, 1 teaspoon salt and some black pepper. Pour over the meat and onion mixture in the casserole. Stir, cover tightly and transfer to a preheated low oven, 140°C (275°F, Gas mark 1), for 2½ –3 hours. Check occasionally and stir in the remaining stock if the mixture seems dry.

At the end of this time, the meat should be tender. Skim off any excess fat, then taste and correct the seasoning, if necessary. Pour into a deep pie dish.

Dust a work surface lightly with flour and roll out the pastry. Use it to cover the dish, decorating the pie as desired. Brush with beaten egg, cream or milk.

Bake the pie in a preheated hot oven, 220°C (425°F, Gas mark 7), for 15 minutes to raise and set the pastry, then reduce the heat to 180°C (350°F, Gas mark 4) and cook for another 30 minutes, until the filling is thoroughly hot.

Meat & Potato Pie with Venison

Meat and tatie (potato) pie was a standby of my grandmother's, a frugal dish that stretched a relatively small amount of meat round a large family. Similar pies remain popular in the textile belt of south-west Yorkshire and south-east Lancashire. This is an upmarket version.

serves 4

450g (1lb) stewing venison, cut into dice
pinch of nutmeg
1 garlic clove, sliced
100g (3½oz) shallots, cut into slices
75ml (2½fl oz) good stock made from venison or beef bones
20g (¾oz) butter
1 tablespoon chopped parsley

1 teaspoon chopped rosemary
1 teaspoon chopped thyme
750g (1lb 10oz) potatoes, peeled and sliced thinly
1 quantity shortcrust pastry (see page 212)
salt and black pepper

Put the venison in the base of a deep pie dish. Season with ½ teaspoon salt, some coarsely ground black pepper and grated nutmeg. Add the garlic and shallots and pour over the stock. Cover with buttered greaseproof paper or some lightly greased foil. Cook in a preheated oven, 160°C (325°F, Gas mark 3), for 1½ hours.

At the end of this time, put the butter in a large frying pan and heat it just enough to melt it. Turn off the heat and stir in the chopped herbs and ½ teaspoon salt. Stir in the sliced potatoes. Remove the meat from the oven and spread the potato mixture over the top. Replace the paper or foil cover and return to the oven on the same temperature for another 1–1½ hours.

To finish the pie, roll out the pastry. Remove the dish of meat and potatoes from the oven, turning the heat up to 200°C (400°F, Gas mark 6) as you do so. Give it a few minutes to cool a little, then cover the pie with the pastry. Crimp the edges and cut a hole for the steam to escape. Return to the oven for 15–20 minutes to set and brown the pastry.

Serve hot with some steamed broccoli, or shredded cabbage cooked with a little bacon and a few juniper berries.

Fish Pie

This fish pie is the type that was common in British cookery during the twentieth century, with mashed potato on top. It's a comforting dish when well made. This version uses a sauce recipe derived from French cookery, which is particularly good.

serves
4

800–900g (1lb 12oz–2lb) floury
  potatoes, cut into chunks
25g (1oz) butter
50ml (2fl oz) milk
55–60g (2–2¼oz) coarsely grated
  cheese – Gruyère for a mild flavour,
  or strong Cheddar
600g (1lb 5oz) cod or haddock fillet
250g (9oz) shell-on prawns

for making stock
the skin and any bones from the fish
the shells from the prawns
150ml (5fl oz) white wine

2 celery stalks, washed and cut into
  1cm (½in) lengths
about 6cm (2½in) of the green leaves
  from a leek, cut into thick slices
a few sprigs parsley
a small carrot, scrubbed and cut
  into quarters
750ml (1¼ pints) water

for the sauce
25g (1oz) butter
25g (1oz) flour
85g (3oz) creme fraîche
salt and black pepper

Put all the ingredients for the stock into a pan and bring to the boil, then reduce the heat and simmer for 25–30 minutes. Strain, discarding the debris.

Make the sauce, melt the butter, stir in the flour and cook for a moment without browning. Stir in about 300ml (10fl oz) of the fish stock to make a smooth sauce. Allow to cook gently for 5–10 minutes, adding a little more stock if it seems on the thick side (the remainder of the stock can be frozen if you have no immediate use for it). Add the creme fraîche and season with salt and pepper to taste.

In the meantime, boil the potatoes until tender, drain and mash with the butter, milk and cheese. Season with salt and pepper to taste.

Cut the fish into slices, 2cm (¾in) wide, and place in a deep ovenproof dish. Add the prawns and pour in the sauce. Top with the mashed potato. Use a fork to roughen the surface. Bake at 190°C (375°F, Gas mark 5) for 30–40 minutes.

Trout Pie

The eighteenth-century recipe given by Martha Bradley (1756), which inspired this idea, required six trout, each weighing about 900g (2lb). It must have been quite a pie. It also demanded eels and freshwater crayfish, both now very difficult to obtain unless you know a keen fisherman or are on good terms with fishmongers who supply restaurants. I've pushed the recipe away from the rich, savoury eighteenth-century style towards the current fashion for south-east Asian flavours, adapting to changing tastes and available ingredients just as people did in the past.

serves 4–6

6 trout, each weighing approximately 300g (11oz)
½ teaspoon salt
1 tablespoon each of chopped fresh coriander, basil, chives
300ml (10fl oz) strong fish stock
1 tablespoon fresh root ginger matchsticks
2 kaffir lime leaves
2cm (¾in) lemongrass, thinly sliced

1 hot red chilli, seeds removed, thinly sliced
140–200g (5–7oz) uncooked king prawns, peeled

for the pie crust
a little butter, for greasing
flour, for dusting
1 quantity puff pastry (see page 214)
beaten egg, cream or milk, for glazing

Ask the the fishmonger to remove the heads and tails of the trout and fillet them. Trim off any fins and wipe the fish well. Reserve the four largest ones.

Skin the other two and blend them with the salt in a food processor to make a paste. Stir in the chopped herbs. Divide this mixture between the four whole fish, folding them over to enclose the stuffing.

Take a deep pie dish and butter it well. Lay the stuffed trout in it. Dust the work surface lightly with flour and roll the pastry out to about 5mm (¼in) thick, then use it to cover the dish. Brush the pastry with some beaten egg, cream or milk.

Bake in a preheated hot oven, 220°C (425°F, Gas mark 7), for 15 minutes to rise and set the pastry, then reduce the heat to 180°C (350°F, Gas mark 4) and cook for another 15 minutes. Remove the pie from the oven.

Heat the fish stock in a pan with the ginger, lime leaves, lemongrass and chilli. When it comes to the boil, add the prawns. Simmer for 3–4 minutes until the prawns are cooked through – stir occasionally so that they cook evenly.

Cut through the edge of the pastry and lift it off. Pour the prawn mixture on top of the trout. Cut the pastry into neat wedges and use to garnish the pie. Serve hot with a green vegetable accompaniment.

Root Vegetable Pie

The original version of this recipe was Woolton Pie, which became infamous during World War II. It was a dish of root vegetables, such as swede and parsnip, cooked under an oatmeal pie crust – plain as plain could be and apparently much disliked by a nation desperate for meat and other luxuries. I thought it would be interesting to update it with more unusual vegetables.

serves
4

300g (11oz) Jerusalem artichokes
300g (11oz) celeriac
300g (11oz) leek (white part only)
300g (11oz) waxy potatoes (such as
    Anya, Pink Fir Apple)
115g (4oz) well-flavoured cheese –
    a good Cheddar, or try Blue Stilton,
    cut into thin slices or crumbled
40g (1½oz) butter

40g (1½oz) flour, plus a little extra
    for rolling out the pastry
600ml (1 pint) milk
pinch of nutmeg
1 quantity puff pastry (see page 234)
beaten egg, cream or milk, to glaze
salt and black pepper

Wash the Jerusalem artichokes, put them in a pan, cover with water and simmer for 10–15 minutes, or until just tender. Drain well and cover them with cold water; once they are cool enough to handle, peel off the papery skin. Cut the flesh into julienne strips. Wash and peel the celeriac and cut into julienne strips. Wash the leek and slice into thin rings. Wash the potatoes, peel them if desired, and then cut into julienne strips.

Put the artichokes in a deep dish, scatter over about one-quarter of the cheese, and repeat with the other vegetables and remainder of the cheese.

Melt the butter in a pan, stir in the flour, then gradually add the milk, stirring all the time, to make a smooth sauce. Season with salt, pepper and a scrape of nutmeg. Pour this over the vegetables in the dish.

Use the extra flour to lightly dust a work surface and roll out the pastry. Use it to cover the dish, trimming it neatly and making some decorative leaves as desired. Make a hole for steam to escape and brush with beaten egg, cream or milk. Cook in a preheated hot oven, 220°C (425°F, Gas mark 7), for 20 minutes, then turn the heat down to 180°C (350°F, Gas mark 4) and cook for a further 40 minutes.

Chestnut & Shallot Pie

This recipe began as an attempt to make a vegetarian equivalent of my grandmother's meat and potato pie, a plain but comforting dish of the farmhouse and urban industrial communities in Yorkshire and Lancashire. Along the way, it developed into something much richer. If you are not concerned with being strictly vegetarian, you can add about 55g (2oz) pancetta cubes, well fried and drained of their fat, to the chestnut and shallot mixture.

serves 4–6

25g (1oz) butter, plus extra for
   the potatoes
200g (7oz) shallots, peeled
8 garlic cloves, peeled
200g (7oz) cooked peeled chestnuts
   (use vacuum packed ones)
2 tablespoons brandy
1 tablespoon chopped parsley
leaves from 1 sprig rosemary, chopped
leaves from 5–6 sprigs thyme

75ml (2½fl oz) single cream
2 tablespoons truffle paste (optional)
50ml (2fl oz) water
800g (1lb 12oz) potatoes, peeled
   and sliced
1 quantity puff pastry (see page 214)
flour, for dusting
beaten egg, cream or milk,
   for glazing
salt and black pepper

Melt the butter in a large frying pan. Add the shallots and fry gently until they begin to develop golden brown patches. Add the garlic and cook for a few moments longer. Add the chestnuts and pour in the brandy. Allow it to bubble, then stir in the herbs and cream. Add the truffle paste, if using, plus the water. Taste and add salt and pepper as desired.

Put the vegetable mixture in the bottom of a deep pie dish. Layer the sliced potatoes over the top, dotting a little butter between them and sprinkling lightly with salt. Lightly dust a work surface with flour and roll out the pastry to about 5mm (¼in) thick. Use this to cover the pie, and decorate the top with pastry leaves, if desired. Cut a hole for the steam to escape, and then brush with beaten egg, cream or milk. Start the pie off in a preheated hot oven, 220°C (425°F, Gas mark 7), for 20 minutes, then turn the heat down to 180°C (350°F, Gas mark 4) and cook for another 40 minutes, or until the potatoes feel done when tested with a small knife through the steam hole. A salad of peppery or bitter leaves, such as watercress or rocket, is good with this.

Hot puddings

Apple Cobs

Also known as Bombard'd Apples or Apple Dumplings. In the original recipe the dumplings were boiled, but here they are baked. Use a really good-quality cooking apple that will go soft and puffy when it's cooked. You can use shortcrust or puff pastry instead of suet-crust pastry if you want a less rich pudding.

serves 6

350g (12oz) self-raising flour
pinch of salt
175g (6oz) suet
50g (1¾oz) caster sugar
about 150ml (5fl oz) ice-cold water
6 medium Bramley apples

2 tablespoons mincemeat
6 cloves
water or milk, for brushing
1 egg white, beaten
3 tablespoons clotted cream
  (optional)

Sieve the flour and salt together into a mixing bowl. Mix in the suet and stir in half the sugar. Add just sufficient water to mix to a soft but not sticky dough. Turn out on to a lightly floured board and divide into 6 equal pieces. Roll out each piece thinly into a square large enough to encase an apple.

Peel and core the apples and place one in the centre of each pastry square. Fill each apple centre with mincemeat and top with a clove. Brush the edge of each pastry square with a little water or milk, draw up the corners to meet over the centre of each apple and press the edges firmly together. Turn upside-down, and place on a greased baking tray. Roll out the pastry trimmings to make small leaves to decorate the dumplings, then brush all over with the beaten egg white and sprinkle with the remaining sugar.

Bake in the centre of a preheated oven, 200°C (400°F, Gas mark 6), for 30 minutes or until golden brown. Remove from the oven and leave to stand for a few minutes on a warm serving dish. Cut a hole in the top of each dumpling and spoon in some clotted cream, or serve with Vanilla Custard Sauce (see page 220).

Gingerbread & Pear Upside-down Pudding

This was a popular pudding in Victorian days and it looks very attractive as well as tasting delicious. You can bake it in a round or a square cake tin.

serves 6

50g (1¾oz) butter
140g (5oz) soft brown sugar
3 firm pears
6 glacé cherries
6 walnut halves
115g (4oz) margarine
115g (4oz) black treacle
115g (4oz) golden syrup
225g (8oz) plain flour

¼ teaspoon salt
pinch of ground cloves
2 teaspoons ground cinnamon
2 teaspoons ground ginger
¼ teaspoon grated nutmeg
1 level teaspoon bicarbonate of soda
150ml (5fl oz) warm
　full-cream milk
2 eggs

Line the bottom and sides of a 20cm (8in) round cake tin with buttered greaseproof paper. Melt the butter in a saucepan over gentle heat, then add 70g (2½oz) brown sugar and stir for a few minutes until dissolved. Pour into the bottom of the tin. Peel, halve and core the pears and put a glacé cherry in the centre of each pear half. Arrange the pears in a circle, cut-side down, on the butter-and-sugar mixture with their stalk ends facing the centre of the tin. Place the walnut halves, cut-side down, between the pears.

Put the margarine, black treacle, golden syrup and remaining brown sugar in a saucepan and melt over a low heat. Sieve flour, salt and spices together into a mixing bowl. Dissolve soda in warm milk. Beat eggs and add to milk mixture when it has cooled a little. Make a well in the centre of the dry ingredients and pour in melted treacle mixture, followed by egg mixture. Stir together and beat thoroughly until a smooth batter is formed. Pour carefully over the pears and walnuts. Bake in the centre of a preheated oven, 180°C (350°F, Gas mark 4), for 40–50 minutes or until well risen and firm (test with a skewer; it should come out clean). Remove from the oven and allow to shrink a little before turning out on to a warmed serving plate. Take great care when peeling off the greaseproof paper. Serve warm with cream or Vanilla Custard Sauce (see page 220).

Plum & Cinnamon Crumble

Crumbles can be varied, not just by using seasonal fruit but also by changing the crumble topping, adding porridge oats (as here), dessicated coconut, chopped nuts, different spices and so on. Classic combinations such as rhubarb and ginger, apple and cinnamon, gooseberry and elderflower, can always be relied on. This particular recipe was given to me by a good friend, who is chef at Cotehele, a medieval house belonging to the National Trust on the banks of the River Tamar, in Cornwall. He cooks the crumble in individual dishes under the grill.

serves 4

600g (1 lb 5oz) English plums, stoned
50g (1¾oz) light brown sugar
½ teaspoon ground cinnamon

for the topping
40g (1½oz) butter, cut in small pieces
55g (2oz) plain flour
½ teaspoon cinnamon
40g (1½oz) light brown sugar
55g (2oz) porridge oats

Poach the plums with the sugar and cinnamon and a very little water until just tender. Remove from the heat and tip into a buttered ovenproof baking dish.

Rub the butter into the flour and cinnamon sieved together in a mixing bowl until the mixture resembles breadcrumbs. Stir in the sugar and oats.

Sprinkle the crumble mixture evenly over the plums and then bake in a moderate preheated oven, 180°C (350°F, Gas mark 4), for about 25 minutes, or until golden brown. Remove from the oven and leave to cool a little.

Eat warm and serve with Vanilla Custard Sauce (see page 22), Vanilla Ice Cream (see page 188) or clotted cream.

Bread & Butter Pudding

Bread and Butter Pudding was in the recipe books by the 1720s, when it was made of freshly sliced and buttered bread with currants, beaten eggs and nutmeg. It was only in Victorian times that it became a means of putting stale bread to good use. Since then it has become a British institution and there are dozens of versions. Modern recipes sometimes add fresh or poached fruit, marmalade, apricot jam or chocolate and use brioche, fruit loaf, panettone and croissants. I love a Bread and Butter Pudding with a high proportion of rich custard to bread.

serves 6

300ml (10fl oz) full-cream or
    Jersey milk
300ml (10fl oz) double cream
1 vanilla pod, split in half
    lengthways
4–6 slices cut from a good-quality
    white sandwich loaf

about 100g (3½oz) butter, softened
55g (2oz) sultanas, soaked in hot water
25g (1oz) candied peel, chopped
3 large eggs
about 70g (2½oz) caster sugar
freshly grated nutmeg
icing sugar, for dredging

Slowly heat the milk and cream with the vanilla pod, including its scraped-out seeds, until boiling point is just reached. Take off the heat and leave to cool a little.

Remove the crusts from the bread and butter generously. Cut each slice into 4 triangles, then arrange, overlapping in the base of a well-buttered 1.5 litre (2¾ pint) ovenproof dish. Sprinkle with the soaked and drained sultanas and peel.

Whisk the eggs with the sugar, then pour into a jug with the strained milk and cream mixture. Taste and add more sugar, if you wish. Whisk again, then carefully pour evenly over the bread, making sure that each triangle gets a good soaking (add more milk if the liquid doesn't cover the bread). Grate plenty of nutmeg over the surface, cover and leave to soak for at least 2 hours, preferably overnight, in the refrigerator. When ready to cook, place the dish in a roasting tin filled with hot water to the level of the top of the custard.

Bake in a preheated oven, 150°C (300°F, Gas mark 2), for 1–1¼ hours until just set and golden (after 30 minutes' cooking time, dredge with icing sugar to crisp up the top). Rest for 20 minutes before serving. No extra cream is really necessary because the custard is very rich and delicious.

Old-fashioned Bread Pudding

In Plymouth, this very old pudding is called Nelson's Cake after the great man who was obviously a lover of it. It is also particularly popular in East Anglia, where Nelson was born. The original version would have been boiled but it is now more commonly baked. Individual bread puddings were fashionable in Georgian times – they were baked in buttered teacups.

serves
4

225g (8oz) stale white or brown
    bread, with crusts removed
300ml (10fl oz) milk
2 tablespoons brandy (optional)
50g (1¾oz) melted butter or suet
50g (1¾oz) soft brown sugar
2 level teaspoons mixed spice

1 egg, beaten
175g (6oz) mixed dried fruit
zest of 1 lemon
zest of ½ orange
freshly grated nutmeg
caster sugar, for sprinkling

Break the bread into small pieces and put in a mixing bowl. Pour over the milk and brandy, if using, stir well and leave to soak for at least 30 minutes.

Add the melted butter or suet, sugar, spice and egg then, using a fork, beat out any lumps. Stir in the dried fruit and grated lemon and orange zest, then turn the mixture into a buttered 1.2 litre (2 pint) ovenproof dish. Grate a little fresh nutmeg over the top.

Bake in a preheated oven, 180°C (350°F, Gas mark 4), for 1¼–1½ hours until the pudding is nicely brown on top. Serve hot, sprinkled with caster sugar and with Vanilla Custard Sauce (see page 220).

Old-fashioned Iced Bread Pudding

Make as above but remove from the oven after 1 hour. Cover with meringue made from 2 egg whites and 115g (4oz) caster sugar. Put back in the oven and cook for a further 20 minutes, or until the meringue is crisp and lightly browned.

Cherry Batter

This famous pudding from Kent has been eaten at cherry feasts and fairs since the thirteenth century, but probably the idea of combining cherries with batter was brought the UK by the Normans. This is a reminder that Kent was one of the first counties to be colonised by them. Kent's famous juicy black morello cherries, said to be the best black cherries in the world, should be used to make this delicious pud, but drained canned black cherries can be used out of season.

serves 6

50g (1¾oz) plain flour
pinch of salt
50g (1¾oz) caster sugar
2 eggs
300ml (10fl oz) milk
1 tablespoon cherry brandy or

a few drops of vanilla essence
25g (1oz) melted butter
450g (1lb) ripe black cherries,
stoned
butter, for dotting
icing sugar, for dredging

Sieve the flour and salt together into a bowl. Stir in the caster sugar. Beat the eggs and blend gradually into flour mixture. Warm the milk and add slowly to the flour mixture, beating vigorously to make a smooth light batter. Stir in the cherry brandy or vanilla essence and whisk in the melted butter. Put aside to rest while you stone the cherries.

Generously butter a shallow 600ml (1 pint) ovenproof porcelain dish or a 20cm (8in) flan tin. Spread the prepared cherries over the bottom of the dish or tin and carefully pour over the batter. Dot with a few tiny pieces of butter and bake in the centre of a preheated oven, 200°C (400°F, Gas mark 6), for 20 minutes, then reduce the temperature to 190°C (375°F, Gas mark 5) and cook for a further 20 minutes or until the batter is well risen and golden, but still creamy inside.

Serve warm, generously dredged with sieved icing sugar and with whipped cream or Vanilla Custard Sauce (see page 220). If you want to serve the pudding cold, remove from the dish or tin and serve with either pouring or whipped cream.

Apricot Amber Pudding

Traditionally, an Amber Pudding was made with apples and baked in a puff-pastry case. It is a very old-fashioned sweet dating back to the eighteenth century, and can be made with many other fruits, such as apples, rhubarb, gooseberries, blackberries, blackcurrants or plums.

**serves
6**

175g (6oz) shortcrust pastry
   (see page 212)
450g (1lb) fresh apricots
150g (5½oz) caster sugar
1 teaspoon lemon juice

25g (1oz) unsalted butter
2 eggs, separated
pinch of salt
crystallized apricot and
   angelica to decorate

Preheat the oven to 200°C (400°C, Gas mark 6), with a large baking sheet in the oven to warm up as well. Roll out the pastry thinly and use to line a buttered 20cm (8in) shallow ovenproof dish. Chill in the refrigerator for 30 minutes. Prick the base and line with baking paper and baking beans. Place in the oven on the hot baking sheet and bake blind for about 10 minutes, then remove the baking parchment and beans and cook for about another 10 minutes to dry out the inside without browning the pastry.

Meanwhile, wash and stone the apricots, then poach in a little water until tender. Rub the fruit through a plastic sieve, then sweeten with about 40g (1½oz) sugar or to taste, adding the lemon juice. Stir in the butter, and beat in the egg yolks. Leave on one side to cool.

Pour the cooled apricot mixture into the cooked pastry case and cook for 20 minutes in the preheated oven at 200°C (400°F, Gas mark 6).

Whisk the egg whites with the salt until stiff, but not dry. Add 55g (2oz) caster sugar and whisk until stiff again. Fold in another 55g (2oz) sugar gently. Reduce the oven temperature to 180°C (350°F, Gas mark 4). Pile the meringue on top of the apricot mixture and spread out, making sure that it touches the edges of the pastry. Dredge with extra caster sugar and bake in the centre of the oven for 20 minutes, or until the meringue is crisp and very lightly browned. Serve warm or cold with whipped cream and decorated with pieces of crystallized apricot and candied angelica, if you wish.

Rich Bakewell Pudding

There are several 'original' recipes in Derbyshire for this famous pudding, but generally it is accepted that it was probably first made by a cook at the Rutland Arms in Bakewell 200 years ago. The original recipe was made in a special oval tin 7.5cm (3in) deep and 15cm (6in) wide and had a thick layer of preserved fruit, such as peaches or apricots, and strips of candied citron or orange peel spread over the pastry. A custard made with eggs, butter and sugar and flavoured with what the Bakewellians call 'lemon brandy' (brandy flavoured with lemon zest) was poured on top of the preserved fruit and the pudding was baked. Ratafia or almond flavouring is more commonly used now, and flaky or rich shortcrust pastry can be used instead of shortcrust.

serves 6

175g (6oz) shortcrust pastry
3 heaped tablespoons home-made or
    good-quality apricot jam
25g (1oz) candied peel, chopped
3 eggs
115g (4oz) caster sugar

115g (4oz) unsalted butter
½ teaspoon vanilla extract or
    ratafia flavouring
1 tablespoon brandy
115g (4oz) ground almonds
sieved icing sugar, for dredging

Roll out the pastry on a lightly floured work surface and use to line a buttered 20cm (8in) oval pie dish. Chill, then bake blind in the usual way (see Apricot Amber Pudding, page 130)in a preheated oven, 200°C (400°F, Gas mark 6). Spread the jam evenly over the cooled pastry case and sprinkle with the peel.

Beat the eggs and sugar together until pale and thick. Melt the butter and run into the egg mixture. Beat together well. Stir in the vanilla essence or ratafia and brandy. Fold in the ground almonds. Pour the mixture over the jam and candied peel in the pastry case. Bake in the centre of the preheated oven, 180°C (350°F, Gas mark 4), for about 30 minutes, or until the filling is set and golden brown. Dredge with sieved icing sugar and serve hot, warm or cold with pouring cream.

Jam Roly-Poly

This popular old-fashioned pudding used to be boiled in a cloth or shirtsleeve, but baking gives the pastry a lovely crisp crust, which is usually more popular with children. Mincemeat or golden syrup can be used instead of jam.

serves 4–6

225g (8oz) self-raising flour
1 teaspoon mixed spice (optional)
pinch of salt
115g (4oz) suet
about 8 tablespoons water

4–5 tablespoons good-quality
   jam, warmed
milk, for brushing
1 egg, beaten, to glaze
caster sugar, for sprinkling

Sieve the flour, spice (if using) and salt together into a mixing bowl. Stir in the suet and add just enough water to mix to a soft, but not sticky, dough. Turn out on to a lightly floured board and roll into a rectangle about 20 x 30cm (8 x 12in). Spread evenly with warm jam, leaving a 1cm (½in) border all the way around. Fold this border over the jam and brush with milk. Roll up fairly loosely and press the edges of the dough together to seal them. Put in a lightly buttered roasting tin and brush with the beaten egg. Sprinkle with caster sugar.

Bake in the centre of a preheated oven, 200°C (400°F, Gas mark 6), with the tin propped up so that the roly-poly rolls into one end, which helps to keep its shape. Cook for 35–40 minutes or until golden brown.

Serve the roly-poly warm, sprinkled with extra caster sugar, and Vanilla Custard Sauce (see page 220).

Roly-poly with Blueberries
Make the roly-poly as before, but fill with 300g (11oz) fresh blueberries mixed with 1 tablespoon flour, 4 tablespoons caster sugar and the juice of 1 lemon or lime. Try other seasonal soft fruits and serve with Vanilla Custard Sauce (see page 220), Vanilla Ice Cream (see page 188) or thick cream

Apple Fritters

serves 6

115g (4oz) plain flour
pinch of salt
½ teaspoon ground cinnamon
150ml (5fl oz) tepid water
2 tablespoons orange liqueur
1 tablespoon vegetable oil
4 medium cooking or crisp
    dessert apples
grated zest and juice of ½ lemon

50g (1¾oz) icing sugar
25g (1oz) caster sugar
6 tablespoons apricot jam or thick
    orange marmalade
2 tablespoons water
fat for deep-frying (lard or oil)
2 egg whites
caster sugar for dredging
orange or lemon segments, for serving

Sieve the flour, salt and cinnamon together into a basin. Make a well in the centre. Gradually blend in the tepid water and 1 tablespoon liqueur, followed by the oil. Beat vigorously with a rotary hand or electric whisk to make a smooth, glossy batter. Cover and leave to stand in a cool place for at least 30 minutes, to allow the starch grains in the flour to absorb the water and swell.

Peel, core and slice the apples in 5mm (¼in) thick slices. Mix together the lemon zest and juice, 1 tablespoon liqueur and sieved icing sugar. Add the apple slices and coat evenly. In a heavy saucepan, dissolve the caster sugar and jam over a low heat. Dilute with water to make a syrup of coating consistency. Simmer the syrup for 1 minute and keep warm. Coat each soaked apple ring in this syrup, allowing any excess to drain off. Leave the apple rings on one side to dry out a little.

When ready to cook the fritters, heat the fat for deep-frying – when a blue vapour rises from the fat, it is hot enough. Test by dropping in a little batter, which will rise if the fat is the correct temperature; if not, the batter will sink. Make sure your fat is absolutely clean and at least 7.5cm (3in) deep. Whisk the egg whites until very stiff and fold into the prepared batter. Using cooking tongs or a long skewer, dip the apple rings, one at a time, into the batter, allowing any excess to drain off. Lower carefully into the hot fat and deep-fry until crisp and puffed, turning them over once or twice. Avoid frying too many at once, because this cools the fat and does not allow room for the fritters to expand properly. When cooked, remove from the fat and drain on crumpled kitchen paper. Serve immediately, dredged with caster sugar, and thick cream or with Orange or Lemon Sauce (see page 221).

Traditional Lemon Pancakes

Although probably not of British origin, pancakes have been established here for so many centuries that they may be considered a national institution. When Lent was strictly observed, eggs and fatty foods were forbidden for forty days and so pancake-making became associated with Shrove Tuesday in the UK, to use up any remaining eggs, butter and milk before the fasting.

makes
10

115g (4oz) plain flour
pinch of salt
zest of 1 lemon
1 egg
300ml (10fl oz) milk
15g (½oz) melted butter, plus
    extra for frying
caster sugar, for sprinkling
2 lemons, for serving

Sieve the flour and salt together into a basin. Stir in the lemon zest. Make a well in the centre and break in the egg. Beat well, incorporating the flour, and add half the milk very gradually, beating all the time until a smooth batter is formed. Add the remaining milk, a little at a time, and beat until well mixed. Leave to stand for at least 30 minutes.

Stir the melted butter into the batter just before cooking. Heat a very little butter in a pancake or omelet pan until very hot. Spoon in a tablespoon of batter and tip the pan until the batter covers its base. Cook until golden brown underneath. Turn over with a palette knife and cook the other side until golden. Turn out on to sugared greaseproof paper, sprinkle with caster sugar and a squeeze of lemon juice. Serve immediately with extra sugar and lemon wedges, or keep warm in the oven until you are ready to serve.

Sweet Apple Omelet

The ancestor of the British omelet, known as a 'herbolace', was a mixture of eggs and shredded herbs baked in a buttered dish. Cheese and milk were added later. This herbolace was replaced by the French 'omelette' in the fourteenth century, referred to in many English recipes as an 'aumelette' or 'alumelle', which gradually became omelet.

serves
4

2 large cooking apples
115g (4oz) butter
115g (4oz) caster sugar
2 tablespoons apple brandy or rum

150ml (5fl oz) double
    or whipping cream
5 eggs
pinch of salt

Peel, core and slice the apples. Fry the apples gently in 50g (1¾oz) butter, turning frequently until tender. Remove from the heat and stir in 50g (1¾oz) caster sugar, the apple brandy and double or whipping cream.

Separate 2 of the eggs and beat the egg yolks and 3 whole eggs together – keep the whites. Add a pinch of salt and 25g (1oz) caster sugar. Whisk the 2 egg whites until stiff and gently fold into the egg mixture.

In a frying pan, melt the remaining butter. When light brown in colour, pour in the egg mixture and cook over a moderate heat, mixing it well with a fork to allow the uncooked egg to run on to the bottom of the hot pan. Cook until golden brown on the bottom and cooked on the top (sweet omelets, unlike savoury omelets, should not be runny on the top).

Spread the apple mixture over the top, fold in half and slide on to a warmed plate. Sprinkle with the remaining caster sugar and caramelize by placing the omelet under a very hot grill for a few minutes.

Another attractive way of finishing this omelet is to heat a skewer until it is red hot and then very carefully draw it over the top of the sugar-sprinkled omelet in a criss-cross pattern.

Puffed Strawberry Omelet

A fluffy sweet omelet flavoured with orange zest and orange-flower water and filled with fresh strawberries. This kind of omelet was eaten as a popular treat over 100 years ago.

serves
2

3 eggs, separated
2 level teaspoons caster sugar
zest of 1 orange
½ teaspoon orange-flower water
   (optional)
2 tablespoons water

15g (½oz) butter
225g (8oz) sliced strawberries
25g (1oz) icing sugar, sifted
1 tablespoon Grand Marnier
   (optional)

Whisk the egg whites with the caster sugar until stiff, but not dry. Beat the egg yolks, orange zest, orange-flower water, if using, and water until creamy. Melt the butter in an omelet or small frying pan over a low heat. Fold the egg whites carefully into the yolks, using a metal spoon. Be careful not to overmix.

Tilt the omelet pan to coat the sides with butter. Pour in the egg mixture. Cook over a moderate heat until golden brown underneath and just firm to touch in the centre. Place under a pre-heated grill and cook until just set. Spread with the sliced strawberries and sprinkle with sifted icing sugar. Fold the omelet and slide gently on to a hot serving plate. Dredge with more icing sugar.

Warm the Grand Marnier, if using, in a small saucepan, pour over the omelet and set alight. Take it to table immediately while the omelet is still flaming. Serve with sweetened whipped cream.

Puffed Lemon Omelet
Replace 1 tablespoon of the water with lemon juice, and use lemon zest instead of orange. Omit the orange-flower water and add a little more caster sugar. Serve without the strawberry filling. Set alight with brandy if you like.

Quire of Paper

Much admired by seventeenth- and eighteenth-century cooks, a quire of paper was a pile of wafer-thin pancakes. The batter, rich with eggs and cream, was run as thinly as possible over the bottom of a heavy pan and cooked on one side only. The completed pancakes were dredged with caster sugar and laid evenly one upon another until the pile contained twenty. A wine sauce and melted butter were served with the pancakes, which were cut into wedges like a cake.

This recipe will make a pile of about ten thin pancakes, but if you use a smaller 18cm (7in) pan you can make more. The pancakes can be spread individually with jam, jelly or fruit purée and cream.

serves 6

115g (4oz) plain flour
pinch of salt
25g (1oz) caster sugar
2 eggs
2 egg yolks

300ml (10fl oz) single cream
2 tablespoons medium sherry
   or Madeira
unsalted butter, for frying
caster sugar, for sprinkling

Sieve the flour and the salt together into a basin. Stir in the sugar. Make a well in the centre of the flour. Put the eggs and egg yolks into the well and gradually mix the eggs and flour together. Add the cream gradually, beating well until a smooth batter is formed. Stir in the sherry or Madeira to make a thin cream.

Heat a heavy-based pancake or omelet pan, brush with melted butter and add 1 tablespoon of batter. Twist the pan until the bottom is evenly coated with batter and cook until the pancake is golden brown underneath. Remove from the pan or turn over and cook the other side. Keep warm in a clean tea towel.

Make a stack of pancakes, filling them with jam and whipped cream or whatever you choose. Sprinkle liberally with caster sugar. Serve hot, cut into wedges, with Orange or Lemon Sauce (see page 221).

Pears in Nightshirts

serves
6

6 large firm dessert pears
425ml (15fl oz) cider
700g (1lb 9oz) cooking apples
15g (½oz) butter
grated zest of 1 lemon
1 tablespoon lemon juice
2–3 whole cloves

85g–115g (3–4oz) caster sugar
85g (3oz) icing sugar, sifted
6 egg whites
pinch of salt
350g (12oz) caster sugar
25g (1oz) toasted flaked almonds

Peel the pears but leave on the stalks. Put the cider in a saucepan large enough to take the pears. Bring to the boil and lower the pears gently into this liquor, using a slotted spoon. Cover and simmer very gently for 30–35 minutes or until the pears are just tender.

While the pears are cooking, make the apple pulp. Peel, core and slice the apples. Rub the butter over the sides and the bottom of a saucepan. Add the apple slices, lemon zest, lemon juice and cloves. Cover with buttered greaseproof paper and cook over a low heat for about 15 minutes until the apples are soft and any liquid has evaporated. Stir gently from time to time. Remove the cloves and beat the apples to a smooth, thick pulp with a wooden spoon. Add sugar to taste. Pour into a buttered ovenproof dish large enough to take the pears, allowing room for the meringue coating.

Drain the cooked pears and roll each one in sifted icing sugar. Place the pears on top of apple pulp. Whisk the egg whites until very stiff. Add 175g (6oz) caster sugar and whisk until stiff and glossy. Fold in the remaining caster sugar and spread or pipe a thick coating of meringue over the pears.

Bake in a preheated oven, 200°C (400°F, Gas mark 6), for 10–15 minutes or until the meringue is crisp and light brown. Serve immediately, sprinkled with toasted flaked almonds.

Old-fashioned Rice Pudding

In Georgian times a rice pudding could be a very elaborate dish. It was either tied loosely in a cloth, boiled and eaten with melted butter, sugar or salt, or a richer dish including eggs, cream, butter, marrow, currants, brandy, ratafia, nutmeg and candied peel was baked with 'a paste round the edge'. You can flavour your pudding with grated lemon or orange zest, ground cinnamon or grated nutmeg, ½ vanilla pod (split lengthways), a few drops of rose water, a few saffron threads or 1 fresh bay leaf. The important thing is to cook the rice very slowly if it is to achieve that unctuous richness and a buttery brown crust. If you have an Aga or similar stove, leave it in the lowest oven overnight, though you will need to add more milk.

serves 4–6

55g (2oz) short-grain rice
850ml (1½ pints) full-cream milk
25g (1oz) butter, cut into
    little pieces
pinch of salt

55g (2oz) caster sugar or 1 level
    tablespoon clear honey
1 curl of lemon rind
150ml (5fl oz) double cream
freshly grated nutmeg

Put the rice, milk, butter, salt, sugar or honey and lemon rind into a buttered ovenproof dish. Stir well, then add the cream. Stir the mixture again, then grate over plenty of fresh nutmeg.

Place the dish, uncovered, in a preheated slow oven, 140°C (275°F, Gas mark 1), and cook for 3–4 hours, or until just starting to set. As the pudding cools, it will finish cooking in its own heat and thicken. Remove from the oven and leave until just warm, or cold, if you like.

Rice Pudding Meringue
Make a meringue topping with 2 egg whites and 115g (4oz) caster sugar. Pile on top of the rice pudding and return to a hot oven, 200°C (400°F, Gas mark 6), for 10–15 minutes to brown the meringue.

Spicy Ground Rice Pudding

This recipe is based on one by Eliza Acton, one of the best known of the nineteenth-century cookery writers. Eggs are added to make a richer pudding. Pies and puddings were often 'iced' or topped with egg whites as in this recipe.

serves
4–6

40g (1½oz) ground rice or semolina
600ml (1 pint) full-cream milk
strip of lemon peel
1 vanilla pod
1 bay leaf
pinch of ground nutmeg
25g (1oz) caster sugar or
   ½ tablespoon honey

2 eggs, separated
25g (1oz) butter
grated nutmeg or ground cinnamon,
   for sprinkling
115g (4oz) caster sugar

Butter thoroughly a 1.2 litre (2 pint) ovenproof dish. Mix the ground rice or semolina to a smooth paste with a little of the milk in a basin. Boil the rest of the milk with the lemon peel, vanilla pod, bay leaf and pinch of nutmeg. Pour on to the ground rice or semolina, stirring continuously.

Rinse the pan in which the milk was boiled and leave a film of cold water on the bottom. Return the rice and milk and bring slowly to the boil again, stirring all the time, so that it does not burn on the bottom of the saucepan. Cook gently for 10 minutes. Add the sugar or honey. Beat the egg yolks and beat into the rice. Remove the vanilla pod, bay leaf and lemon peel. Pour into the prepared pie dish. Dot with butter and sprinkle with nutmeg or cinnamon.

Bake in the centre of a preheated oven, 180°C (350°F, Gas mark 4), for about 25 minutes. Meanwhile, whisk the egg whites until stiff and whisk in 50g (1¾oz) caster sugar. Fold in the remaining caster sugar. Pile the sweetened egg whites on top of the pudding and bake for a further 20 minutes, until the meringue is crisp and lightly browned. Serve hot with pouring cream and a fruit sauce.

Queen's Pudding

Also called Queen of Puddings, this dish was named after Queen Victoria and was created by her chefs at Buckingham Palace, but it was, in fact, based on a much older seventeenth-century recipe – a milk pudding thickened with breadcrumbs and eggs. It was originally baked in a 'puff paste' case. Try using lemon or lime curd instead of jam.

**serves
6**

85g (3oz) fresh white breadcrumbs
3 eggs, separated
200g (7oz) caster sugar
600ml (1 pint) full-cream milk

25g (1oz) butter
grated zest of ½ lemon
3 tablespoons raspberry jam

Butter a 1.2 litre (2 pint) ovenproof dish. Sprinkle the breadcrumbs into the bottom of the dish. Beat the egg yolks with 25g (1oz) caster sugar. Put the milk, butter and lemon zest in a saucepan and bring slowly to the boil. Cool a little and then pour on to the egg yolks, stirring continuously until the mixture is smooth. Strain the custard over the breadcrumbs and leave to soak for at least 15 minutes.

Stand the dish in a roasting tin half-filled with hot water and bake in the centre of a preheated oven, 180°C (350°F, Gas mark 4), for 25–30 minutes, or until lightly set. Warm the jam and spread over the top of the pudding. Whisk the egg whites until very stiff and add 85g (3oz) caster sugar. Whisk again until stiff and glossy. Fold in the remaining sugar. Pile or pipe the meringue on top of the jam. Sprinkle with extra sugar and bake for a further 15–20 minutes or until the meringue is crisp and lightly browned.

Serve warm, with or without Jam Sauce (see page 221) and pouring cream, or cold with fresh raspberries and cream.

Manchester Pudding

Put a layer of apricot jam in the bottom of an ovenproof dish. Continue as before, but include 2 tablespoons of sherry or brandy in the custard. When the pudding is lightly set, spread with more apricot jam, and top with the meringue as before. Serve warm or cold with pouring cream and poached fresh apricots.

Mucky-mouth Pie

A traditional fruit pie from the north of England made with apples, bilberries and fresh mint. For many centuries the latter was thought to be aphrodisiac, but who knows whether northern housewives were aware of this? Certainly this pie was a favourite with their menfolk. The pastry lid is 'iced' in the traditional way, so the fruit needs to be on the sharp side. If you don't want to use bilberries, blackcurrants, blackberries, blueberries or damsons are all suitable.

serves 6

225g (8oz) shortcrust pastry

for the filling
2 large Bramley apples
450g (1lb) bilberries
a little caster sugar

2 tablespoons fresh mint, finely chopped

for the icing
1 large egg white
115g (4oz) icing sugar

Chill the pastry, then roll out half of it and use it to line a buttered 20cm (8in) pie plate. Prick the base of the pastry, then chill again.

Peel, core and slice the apples and cook them to a purée with a very little water. Mix with the bilberries and chopped mint. Sprinkle with a little sugar – not too much because of the sweet icing on top of the pie. Spoon the fruit mixture into the flan ring or pie plate and roll out the rest of the pastry to make a lid.

Bake the pie in a hot preheated oven, 200°C (400°F, Gas mark 6), for about 25 minutes, then remove from the oven and leave to cool slightly. Reduce the oven temperature to 180°C (350°F, Gas mark 4).

To prepare the icing, whisk the egg white until very stiff, then whisk in the sieved icing sugar until the mixture stands in peaks. Spread thickly over the pie crust and put back in the oven for about 10 minutes, until the icing hardens and is very slightly browned. Serve warm with cream.

Royal Pie

In Elizabethan times a 'royal pye' was any savoury or sweet pie that was 'iced' with sugar and egg white – more like our modern royal icing than meringue, which is its descendant. This particular Royal Pye is filled with mincemeat, apples and grapes and is ideal for serving at Christmas alongside, or instead of, the plum pudding. The rich shortcrust pastry was originally called 'biscuit crust'.

serves 6–8

175g (6oz) sweet shortcrust pastry
  (see Chocolate and Prune Tart
  page 224)

for the filling
450g (1lb) Cox's apples

115g (4oz) seedless green grapes
450g (1lb) homemade or good-quality
  mincemeat
1–2 tablespoons brandy or sherry
2 egg whites
115g (4oz) caster sugar

After making your pastry, chill in the refrigerator for 30 minutes, then roll out and use to line a buttered 23cm (9in) flan tin. Chill again for about 15 minutes. Preheat the oven to 200°C (400°F, Gas mark 6) and bake blind in the usual way (see Apricot Amber Pudding, page 132).

Peel, core and chop the apples. Halve the grapes if large. Mix the apples and grapes with the mincemeat, then stir in the brandy or sherry and spoon the mixture into the pastry case. Cook the pie in the preheated oven at 190°C (375°F, Gas mark 5) for 30 minutes.

Whisk the egg whites until stiff and whisk in half the caster sugar until smooth and glossy. Gently fold in the remaining sugar and pile the meringue on top of the pie. Put back in the oven and bake for a further 15–20 minutes until the meringue is crisp and lightly brown. Serve warm with cream.

Cumberland Rum Nicky

Small versions of this pie, similar to mince pies and called Rum Nickies, can also be made. It recalls the days in the eighteenth century when Whitehaven in Cumbria was one of the leading ports in the rum trade with the West Indies.

serves 6

for the pastry
225g (8oz) plain flour
pinch of salt
115g (4oz) butter
25g (1oz) caster sugar
1 egg yolk
2–3 tablespoons ice-cold water

for the filling
115g (4oz) chopped dates
50g (1¾oz) chopped preserved ginger
50g (1¾oz) butter
25g (1oz) caster sugar
2 tablespoons dark rum
icing sugar, for dredging

Sieve the flour and salt together into a mixing bowl. Rub in the butter until the mixture resembles breadcrumbs. Stir in the sugar. Add the egg yolk and enough ice-cold water to mix to a firm dough. Knead the dough lightly until smooth. Chill for at least 30 minutes.

Roll out the pastry on a lightly floured board. Line a buttered 20cm (8in) pie or ovenproof plate with half the pastry. Sprinkle over the chopped dates and ginger. Cream the butter and the sugar together until pale and fluffy. Beat in the rum gradually. Spread the mixture over the fruit in the pie plate. Cover with the remaining pastry, sealing the edges well. Make a couple of slits in the top of the pastry, flute the edges and decorate as you wish with pastry trimmings.

Bake in the centre of a preheated oven, 200°C (400°F, Gas mark 6), for 10–15 minutes and then reduce the temperature to 180°C (350°F, Gas mark 4) for a further 25–30 minutes. Serve the pie hot, dredged with icing sugar, with some whipped or clotted cream.

Lady's Tart

This nineteenth-century tart was originally filled with apricot preserve and decorated with flaked almonds. It had a decorative edge of small pastry circles. In this recipe, I have used four varieties of jam laid in sections and divided by strips of pastry – once the pride of housewives, who, of course, used their best home-made jams.

serves
6

225g (8oz) shortcrust pastry
  (see page 232)
2 tablespoons apricot jam
2 tablespoons raspberry or
  strawberry jam
2 tablespoons blackcurrant jam
2 tablespoons green gooseberry
  or greengage jam
milk or water, for brushing
1 egg, beaten
1 tablespoon cold water

Roll out the pastry thinly and use two-thirds of it to line a buttered 25cm (10in) ovenproof plate. Divide the pastry base into 8 sections, marking lightly with a knife. Spread each section with the different jams, alternating the colours and avoiding the rim of the plate. Cut the pastry trimmings into narrow strips and arrange in twists across the tart dividing the jams.

Cut the remaining one-third of the pastry into small circles with a 2.5cm (1in) cutter. Brush the rim of the pastry-lined plate with a little milk or water and arrange the circles around the edge, overlapping them a little.

Beat the egg with the water and brush the pastry circles and twists carefully to glaze. Bake in the centre of a preheated oven. 190°C (375°F, Gas mark 5), for about 30 minutes or until the pastry is golden brown. Serve hot or cold with Vanilla Custard Sauce (see page 220) or with thick cream.

Apple Hat

This favourite Victorian suet-crust pudding is filled with apples, raisins and spices. Other seasonal fruits are just as successful – you can try pears, plums, damsons or gooseberries. The dried fruit can be omitted, chopped nuts added and alternative spices used.

serves 6

225g (8oz) self raising flour
pinch of salt
115g (4oz) suet
6–8 tablespoons cold water
675g (1½lb) cooking apples
50g (1¾oz) raisins or sultanas
85g (3oz) brown or white sugar

3 whole cloves
pinch of ground cinnamon
pinch of ground ginger
grated zest and juice of ½ lemon
    or 1 orange
50g (1¾oz) unsalted butter
1 tablespoon clotted cream

Sieve the flour with the salt into a mixing bowl. Stir in the suet and mix with sufficient cold water to make a soft, light dough. Knead lightly and roll out on a floured board about 5mm (¼in) thick. Use two-thirds of the pastry to line a buttered pudding basin.

Peel, core and slice the apples and fill the lined basin with layers of apples, raisins or sultanas, sugar and spices. Add the lemon or orange zest and juice and the butter, cut into small pieces. Cover the basin with the reserved piece of pastry, dampening the edges and pressing together firmly. Cover securely with pleated greaseproof paper and kitchen foil or a pudding cloth and steam for 2–2½ hours.

Turn out on to a warm serving plate and remove a square of the pastry from the top of the pudding. Pop in a tablespoon of clotted cream, which will melt into the pudding. Serve hot with Vanilla Custard Sauce (see page 220).

Apple & Bramble Hat
Use 450g (1lb) cooking apples and 225g (8oz) blackberries. Omit the raisins.

Bachelor's Pudding

2 tablespoons golden syrup
115g (4oz) unsalted butter
115g (4oz) caster sugar
2 eggs
140g (5oz) self-raising flour

2 tablespoons milk or water
450g (1lb) cooking apples
50g (1¾oz) currants
85g (3oz) demerara sugar
1 level teaspoon ground cinnamon

Butter thoroughly a 1.2 litre (2 pint) pudding basin. Pour the golden syrup into
the bottom. Cream the butter and caster sugar together until pale and fluffy. Beat
the eggs and add gradually to the creamed mixture. Fold in the flour gently with
a metal spoon. Add sufficient milk or water to make a soft dropping consistency.

Peel, core and slice the apples and mix with the currants, demerara sugar and
cinnamon. Pour a layer of pudding mixture into the bottom of the basin, top with
an apple layer and then a layer of pudding mixture and the remaining apples.
Spoon over the remaining pudding mixture. Cover securely with some pleated
greaseproof paper and foil and steam for 2–2½ hours until firm and well risen.

Turn out on to a warm serving dish and serve with clotted cream or Vanilla
Custard Sauce (see page 220).

Traditional Christmas Plum Pudding

Plum porridge or pottage was the earliest form of plum pudding and dates back to medieval times. This was made from meat, usually shin of beef and veal, stewed together with currants, raisins, prunes (the dried plums which give their names to the mixture), spices, sugar, sack, lemon juice and claret. The whole thing was thickened with brown breadcrumbs or sago. By the nineteenth century, meat had been left out and the pudding became more like our modern-day Christmas pudding.

The idea of putting silver trinkets and charms into the pudding probably came from the earlier tradition of the beans inside the Twelfth Night Cake, but this has since died out. It is still traditional to bury a silver coin, if you have one, in the mixture. All the family should stir the pudding in turn on Stir-up Sunday, the Sunday before Advent, and make a wish at the same time. The coin should then be pushed in, plus a ring and a thimble; the coin is to bring worldly fortune, the ring a marriage and the thimble a life of blessedness.

makes 5 x 450g (1lb) puddings

225g (8oz) large prunes
300ml (10fl oz) cold tea
225g (8oz) currants
225g (8oz) sultanas
225g (8oz) large raisins
225g (8oz) self-raising flour
¼ teaspoon salt
½ teaspoon baking powder
1 teaspoon mixed spice
½ teaspoon grated nutmeg
½ teaspoon cinnamon
½ teaspoon ground ginger
450g (1lb) fresh white breadcrumbs
225g (8oz) soft dark brown sugar

225g (8oz) shredded suet
50g (1¾oz) candied citron peel, chopped
50g (1¾oz) candied orange and lemon peel, finely chopped
115g (4oz) blanched almonds, chopped
grated zest and juice of 1 orange
grated zest and juice of 1 lemon
115g (4oz) carrot, grated
115g (4oz) cooking apple, grated
300ml (10fl oz) stout
3 eggs, beaten
rum to mix, about 4 tablespoons

Soak the prunes overnight in the cold tea. Next day, drain, remove the stones and chop the prunes finely. The addition of prunes gives a richer, darker colour to the pudding as well as a very good flavour. Wash and dry all the remaining dried fruit and stone the raisins if necessary.

Sieve the flour, salt, baking powder and spices together into a very large bowl. Add the breadcrumbs, sugar and suet, mixing in each ingredient thoroughly. Gradually mix in all the dried fruit, candied peel and almonds. Stir in the zest and juice of the lemon and orange, followed by the grated carrot and apple. Pour in the stout and mix until smooth. Cover the basin with a clean cloth and leave in a cool place overnight or longer if convenient (the flavour will improve). In fact, the mixture can be left to stand for a fortnight or longer at this point. Stir the mixture every day if you decide to do this.

On the day you want to cook the puddings, add the beaten eggs. Stir furiously until the pudding ingredients are thoroughly blended. Add enough rum to make a soft dropping consistency. Spoon the mixture into greased pudding basins to come within 2.5cm (1in) of the rim, packing the mixture down well with the back of a wooden spoon. You will need five 450g (1lb) basins or two 900g (2lb) and one 450g (1lb) basins. Cover the top of each with greased greaseproof paper. Put a thick layer of flour on top of the greaseproof paper, pressing it down well (this will become a solid paste and act as a seal both for cooking and storing). Then cover with another piece of greaseproof paper. Finally, cover the basins with a pudding cloth, muslin or kitchen foil, making a pleat in the centre to allow room for the puddings to rise during cooking. Tie securely with string and make a handle of string across the top of each basin, so that you can lift the puddings in and out of the pan easily.

Place the puddings in a steamer, double boiler, or in a large pan of gently boiling water. Steam for at least 6 hours, topping up the water level from time to time with boiling water. When cooked, remove the puddings from the pan and leave until cold. Renew the top piece of greaseproof paper and cloth and store in a cool, dry place until needed.

On the great day, steam again for 2–3 hours before serving. Turn out the pudding on to a large platter. Sprinkle with icing sugar. Heat some brandy, whisky, rum or Kirsch in a small saucepan or ladle. Pour over the pudding and set alight. Bring the pudding to the table, burning, and surrounded by a neat hedge of holly. Any spirit can be used, but you will find that rum burns for longer. Make sure your holly doesn't go up in smoke!

Spotted Dick

Setting aside the double entendre, the contentious word is thought to be a Huddersfield term for pudding. A Spotted Dick is traditionally made with currants only, but you can use raisins or a mixture of dried fruits if you wish.

225g (8oz) self-raising flour
pinch of salt
115g (4oz) suet, butter or margarine
25g (1oz) caster sugar
175g (6oz) currants, soaked in brandy
about 150ml (5fl oz) full-cream milk

Butter a 1.2 litre (2 pint) pudding basin. Sieve together the flour and salt into the basin, then stir in the suet, or rub in the butter or margarine. Add the sugar and soaked currants. Mix with enough milk to make a soft dropping consistency. Turn into the basin and cover securely with pleated greaseproof paper and kitchen foil or a pudding cloth.

Steam for 2 hours, then serve very hot with Vanilla Custard Sauce (see page 220) or Syrup Sauce (see page 219).

Ginger Spotted Dick

Sieve ½ teaspoon ground ginger with the flour and salt and add 2 pieces of finely chopped preserved ginger to the currants.

Rich Chocolate Pudding

serves 6

85g (3oz) good-quality
   plain chocolate
50g (1¾oz) butter
300ml (½ pint) full-cream milk
50g (1¾oz) caster sugar
2 eggs, separated
½ teaspoon vanilla essence
150g (5½oz) fresh white breadcrumbs

Butter an 850ml (1½ pint) pudding basin well. Melt the chocolate and butter in a basin over a saucepan of hot water (don't be tempted to use cooking chocolate for this pudding – the flavour will not be as good). Remove the chocolate from the heat and stir. Warm the milk in a saucepan and add gradually to the chocolate mixture. Stir in the sugar. Beat the egg yolks and add the vanilla essence. Stir into the chocolate mixture. Add the breadcrumbs. Whisk the egg whites until stiff and fold gently into the pudding mixture.

Turn the pudding mixture into the prepared basin and then cover securely with pleated greaseproof paper and kitchen foil or a pudding cloth. Steam the pudding for 1½–2 hours until well risen and springy.

Serve the pudding hot with Chocolate Orange Sauce (see page 216) or cold with some whipped cream.

Rich Chocolate & Walnut Pudding
Add 85g (3oz) finely chopped walnuts to the pudding mixture.

Rich Chocolate & Orange Pudding
Add the grated zest of 1 orange and ½ lemon and 1 tablespoon brandy.

Golden Syrup Sponge

Still everybody's favourite, this lovely pudding was made widely across the United Kingdom after golden syrup was first produced in the nineteenth century.

serves 6

115g (4oz) butter
115g (4oz) caster sugar
2 eggs
115g (4oz) self-raising flour
pinch of salt
1–2 tablespoons cold water
3 tablespoons golden syrup

Butter an 850ml (1½ pint) pudding basin thoroughly. Cream the butter and sugar together until pale and fluffy. Beat the eggs and add, a little at a time, to the creamed mixture, beating well between each addition. Sieve the flour and salt together and then carefully fold into the sponge mixture, using a metal spoon. Add enough water to make a soft dropping consistency.

Spoon the golden syrup into the buttered basin, then pour on the sponge mixture. Cover securely with pleated greaseproof paper and kitchen foil or a pudding cloth, then steam for 1½–2 hours until well risen and spongy.

Serve hot with Vanilla Custard Sauce (see page 240) or Syrup Sauce (see page 239) or with clotted cream – particularly good for an al fresco summer dinner party in the garden.

Marmalade or Jam Sponge
Replace the golden syrup with good-quality marmalade or jam. Serve with Jam Sauce (see page 221).

Ginger Syrup Sponge
Sieve 1½ teaspoons ground ginger with the flour.

Sussex Pond Pudding

serves 6

175g (6oz) self-raising flour
pinch of salt
1 level teaspoon baking powder
50g (1¾oz) fresh white breadcrumbs
115g (4oz) suet
150ml (5fl oz) or a little more mixed
   cold milk and water
175g (6oz) butter
175g (6oz) demerara sugar
1 large thin-skinned lemon

Sift the flour, salt and baking powder into a mixing bowl. Stir in the breadcrumbs and suet. With a round-bladed knife, mix in milk and water until you have a soft elastic dough. Form the dough into a ball on a floured board. Generously butter a 1.2 litre (2 pint) pudding basin. Cut off about one-quarter of the dough and set aside for the lid. Roll out the large piece of dough into a circle, about 5cm (2in) wider than the top of the pudding basin, and line the basin with this pastry, pressing it firmly to shape.

Cut the butter into rough pieces and put half of it with half the sugar into the pastry-lined basin. Prick the lemon deeply all over with a skewer and lay it on the butter and sugar. Then put the remaining butter and sugar on top. If the mixture is far below the top of the basin you can add some more butter and sugar. Fold the ends of the pastry in over the filling and moisten. Roll out the remaining pastry into a circle to form the lid and lay it on top, pressing the edge to seal.

Cover securely with pleated greaseproof paper and kitchen foil or a pudding cloth and steam for 3½–4 hours, topping up with boiling water if necessary. Turn the pudding out on to a serving dish large enough for the juices to seep out round it. Serve hot with Vanilla Custard Sauce (see page 240) or thick, fresh cream.

Kentish Well Pudding
Pack 115g (4oz) currants around the lemon and continue as before.

Orange & Treacle Sponge Pudding

serves 6

for the sauce
3 tablespoons golden syrup
grated zest and juice of 2 oranges
2 tablespoons fresh white breadcrumbs

for the sponge
115g (4oz) unsalted butter
115g (4oz) caster sugar
2 eggs
115g (4oz) self-raising flour
about 1 tablespoon cold water

Butter an 850ml (1½ pint) pudding basin thoroughly. Put the golden syrup, zest of 1 orange, and juice of 2 oranges in a small heavy saucepan. Warm gently to make a runny sauce. Fold in the breadcrumbs and pour the sauce into the bottom of the prepared basin.

Cream the butter and sugar together until pale and fluffy. Beat the eggs and add, a little at a time, to the creamed mixture. Sieve the flour and gently fold into the mixture using a metal spoon. Stir in the zest of the second orange and enough water to make a soft dropping consistency. Pour the mixture into the prepared basin and cover securely with pleated greaseproof paper and kitchen foil or a pudding cloth. Steam for 1½–2 hours until well-risen and firm.

Turn the pudding out on to a large warm serving plate, allowing room for the sauce. Serve with Orange Sauce (see page 221), Vanilla Custard Sauce (see page 220) or pouring cream.

Cold puddings

Cranachan

This traditional Scottish pudding started life as a hot drink, similar to the Elizabethan version of syllabub, and was later thickened with oatmeal. Fragrant heather honey, Scotch whisky and Scottish raspberries are traditional, but other fruits and alcohol can be used.

serves
4–6

85g (3oz) coarse oatmeal
300ml (10fl oz) double cream
50g (1¾oz) caster sugar
50ml (2fl oz) malt whisky
350g (12oz) fresh raspberries,
    reserving a few for decoration
sprigs of fresh mint

Sprinkle the oatmeal on to a baking tray. Bake in a preheated oven, 200°C (400°F, Gas mark 6), until browned and crisp, moving the oatmeal around to prevent it sticking and burning. Remove from the oven and cool.

Whip the cream with the sugar and whisky, until it stands in fairly soft peaks. Gently fold in the cooled toasted oatmeal. Spoon into individual serving glasses, layering the raspberries between spoonfuls of the creamy mixture, as you go. Serve decorated with a few raspberries and a sprig of fresh mint.

Cranachan with Strawberries

Quarter 600g (1lb 5oz) strawberries and leave to soak in 25g (1oz) caster sugar and 50ml (2fl oz) raspberry liqueur for at least 10 minutes. Gently heat the oatmeal and 50g (1¾oz) soft brown sugar for 2–3 minutes, stirring continuously until the sugar has dissolved and the oatmeal is golden and caramelized. Remove from the heat and spread the oatmeal on a plate to cool, breaking up any large clusters with a fork. Continue as before.

Whim-wham

This Edwardian trifle used Naples biscuits, which were the foundation for many eighteenth- and nineteenth-century desserts, instead of sponge cakes, and syllabub instead of custard. It is very rich, so only serve it in small portions.

serves
6

300ml (10fl oz) double cream
55g (2oz) caster sugar
2 tablespoons white wine
grated zest of 1 lemon
12 sponge finger or boudoir biscuits
225g (8oz) redcurrant, quince or apple jelly
25g (1oz) chopped candied orange peel

Put the cream, sugar, wine and lemon zest into a large mixing bowl and then whisk until really thick to make the syllabub.

Break the biscuits into several pieces and spoon layers of syllabub, biscuits and jelly alternately into an attractive glass seerving bowl, ending with a layer of syllabub. Sprinkle with chopped candied orange peel and chill overnight.

Lemon Posset

A posset was an Elizabethan drink made of milk curdled with sack (sack is the old name of a Spanish wine rather like sherry) or claret, beer, ale and orange or lemon juice – rather like a syllabub. Breadcrumbs were added to thicken the posset in order that it could be eaten rather than drunk. Later, these were omitted and beaten egg whites were used instead to make the dessert lighter and not so rich.

serves 4

600ml (1 pint) double or whipping cream
grated zest of 1½ lemons
150ml (5fl oz) dry white wine
4 tablespoons lemon juice
about 115g (4oz) caster sugar
3 large egg whites
2 tablespoons caster sugar
slivers of lemon zest, for decorating

Beat the cream and lemon zest in a mixing bowl until thick. Beat in the wine until thick again. Add the lemon juice very gradually, beating all the time. Add sugar to taste and beat until stiff.

In a clean, dry bowl, whisk the egg whites until stiff and standing in peaks, then whisk in the 2 tablespoons of sugar until smooth and glossy. Gently fold the egg whites into the cream mixture with a metal spoon, then pile into a large glass or china bowl or individual ramekin dishes. Serve chilled and decorated with lemon zest. Accompany with home-made dessert biscuits.

Orange Posset
Substitute the grated zest of 1 orange for 1 lemon and 2 tablespoons of orange juice for 2 tablespoons of the lemon juice. Decorate with orange zest.

Gooseberry & Elderflower Fool

'Soft, pale, creamy, untroubled, the English fruit fool is the most frail and insubstantial of English summer dishes,' wrote Elizabeth David. The fruit fool, probably named after the French verb *fouler*, meaning 'to crush', is one of the few quintessentially English puddings that should not be tampered with – for me, the perfect fool is just cream, fruit (flavoured or plain) and sugar.

Gooseberry fool has been very popular for centuries, but it was particularly loved by the Victorians, who added egg-thickened custard. In this recipe, I have gone back to basics, although I've flavoured the gooseberries with elderflowers, which are flowering at the same time. If you want to use frozen gooseberries out of season, elderflower cordial can be used instead but with less sugar. The fool mixture can be frozen as an ice cream.

serves
4–6

450g (1lb) green gooseberries
3 or 4 large elderflower heads
    in full bloom
1 tablespoon water
85–115g (3–4oz) caster sugar
300ml (10fl oz) double cream

Wash and top and tail the gooseberries. Put them in a heavy saucepan with the elderflower heads, tied together with cotton thread, the water and the sugar. Cook gently until the fruit is soft and then set aside to cool. Once cool, lift out the elderflower stalks – don't worry about leaving the flowers behind as they will add to the flavour. Mash the gooseberries with a fork and taste for sweetness (if you prefer a smoother purée, rub the gooseberries through a plastic sieve). Leave to get completely cold.

Whip the double cream until thick and just beginning to hold its shape. Gently fold it into the gooseberry purée to give a swirled, marbled effect, then pile into a serving bowl or individual glasses. Decorate the fool with a few small sprigs of elderflower, if in season. Serve with home-made biscuits.

Any fruits can be used to make fools but, for me, the most successful are berries, currants, apricots, the plum family and, of course, rhubarb.

London Syllabub

Syllabub is one of the oldest known British dishes. London Syllabub is one example of a typical Georgian syllabub of the 'everlasting' type, which meant that it didn't separate into a honey-combed curd on the top with an alcoholic drink underneath. Allow the lemon or orange rind and rosemary to infuse in the fruit juice and the alcohol, overnight if possible.

serves
4–6

finely pared rind of 1 lemon
　or 2 oranges
juice of 1 lemon or orange
1 rosemary sprig, bruised
150ml (5fl oz) white wine,
　dry sherry or Madeira

2 tablespoons brandy
85g (3oz) caster sugar or honey
300ml (10fl oz) double cream
fresh rosemary sprigs, for
　decorating

Put the lemon or orange rind and juice and rosemary in a bowl with the wine and brandy and leave overnight. Next day, strain the wine and orange or lemon mixture into a saucepan. Add the sugar or honey and heat gently until the sugar has dissolved. Pour into a large, deep bowl and leave to cool. Gradually stir in the cream, beating until it 'ribbons' and stands in soft peaks (don't use an electric blender or the cream may become grainy). Pour the syllabub into individual glasses, or custard cups, and chill. Serve decorated with sprigs of rosemary. This is also very good with Apple Fritters (see page 134).

Lavender Syllabub
Flavour the syllabub with 2 sprigs of lavender, bruised well, instead of the rosemary. Serve decorated with lavender flowers. Many other herbs and flowers can be used to flavour syllabub. Lemon geranium leaves are also very successful. Use 8 bruised leaves to 300ml (10fl oz) cream.

Spiced Syllabub
Infuse the rind of 1 orange, 1 lemon, 1 stick of cinnamon and 8 cloves in 200ml (7fl oz) good-quality red wine overnight, then continue as before. Serve decorated with orange zest.

Boodles Orange Fool

This is a speciality at Boodles Club in St James' Street, London, which was founded in 1762. It sounds extremely simple but is delicious. The idea of combining sponge with fruit fool dates back to the eighteenth-century version with ratafias.

serves
4–6

4 trifle sponges
grated zest and juice of 1 lemon
grated zest and juice of 2 oranges
55–85g (2–3oz) caster sugar
600ml (1 pint) double cream
crystallized orange peels or slices
crystallized angelica

Cut the sponge cakes into 1cm (½in) strips and line the base of a glass serving dish, or individual glass dishes. Mix the zest and juice of the citrus fruit with the sugar and stir until dissolved. Whip half the cream until thick but not stiff, and beat the juice into the cream slowly. Taste for sweetness.

Spoon the citrus cream over the sponge cakes and chill thoroughly for 2–3 hours, until the juice has soaked into the sponge and the cream has set.

Whip the remaining cream until stiff, and then pipe in attractive swirls on top of the pudding to decorate. Decorate with crystallized fruit and angelica.

Little Chocolate Pots

serves
6

175g (6oz) good-quality plain chocolate
2 tablespoons water
15g (½oz) salted butter
3 eggs, separated

Break the chocolate into small pieces, then put it in a basin with the water. Suspend the basin over a pan of gently simmering water to melt the chocolate into a thick cream, stirring from time to time. Remove from the heat and stir in the butter. Beat in the egg yolks, one at a time (they will be slightly cooked in the hot chocolate mixture). Leave to cool.

Whisk the egg whites in a clean, dry bowl until stiff, then briskly fold into the chocolate mixture. When thoroughly mixed, pour into little custard pots or ramekins. Chill overnight. Serve with home-made dessert biscuits.

Little Chocolate & Orange Pots

Stir the grated zest of 1 large orange and 1 tablespoon orange liqueur into the melted chocolate with the butter.

Little Chocolate & Coffee Pots

Stir 1 tablespoon coffee essence or very strong espresso into the melted chocolate with the butter.

Marmalade Ripple

Any marmalade may be used in this recipe depending on your personal taste, but top-quality thick-cut Seville is too strong except for the most dedicated marmalade lovers.

4 large eggs, separated
1 tablespoon lemon juice
115g (4oz) caster sugar
425ml (15fl oz) double or
    whipping cream
4–8 tablespoons marmalade (to taste)
1 tablespoon orange liqueur

In a bowl, beat the egg yolks with the lemon juice and caster sugar until pale and frothy. Whip the cream until it stands in soft peaks and gently fold into the egg mixture. Whisk the egg whites in a clean, dry bowl until soft and fold gently into the mixture with a metal spoon, distributing them evenly.

Pour into a lidded plastic container and freeze. When the mixture is almost frozen, mix together the marmalade and orange liqueur, then fold into the ice cream to create a gorgeous ripple effect. Replace in the freezer until frozen.

Vanilla Ice Cream

If you want a vanilla ice cream with real flavour, this recipe is for you, but leave the vanilla pod whole if you prefer a more neutral-based ice cream. Use the left-over egg whites for meringues.

serves
6

1 vanilla pod
300ml (10fl oz) full-cream milk
3 large egg yolks
about 115g (4oz) caster sugar
300ml (10fl oz) double cream

Split the vanilla pod lengthways, then, using a knife, strip out the seeds on to a white plate, so that you don't lose any. Put the seeds on one side for later. Put the milk and vanilla pod (without the seeds) into a pan. Bring slowly to the boil, stirring occasionally. Draw off the heat, cover and leave for 20 minutes to infuse.

Whisk the egg yolks in a bowl with the sugar and vanilla seeds, then whisk in the vanilla-infused milk, including the pod. Set the bowl over a pan of gently simmering water and cook, stirring continuously, until the custard thickens and covers the back of a wooden spoon. Taste the custard and add more sugar if you wish. Leave to cool, then strain.

Whip the cream lightly and gently fold into the custard, then pour into a lidded plastic container and freeze. Half an hour before serving, transfer the ice cream to the refrigerator to soften,. This tastes divine if served with Rich Chocolate Pudding (see page 164).

Vanilla & Walnut Ice Cream

The addition of toasted walnuts to the above recipe makes a stunning ice cream. Spread 85g (3oz) chopped walnuts on to a baking tray and toast in a preheated oven, 200°C (400°F, Gas mark 6), for 4–7 minutes, shaking them once or twice. Tip into a metal sieve and shake to dislodge any flakes of papery skin, which should be discarded. Leave to cool. When your ice cream is semi-frozen, fold in the toasted walnuts. Return to the freezer to set solid.

Stem Ginger Ice Cream

This is a delicious ice cream and ideal for serving at Christmas lunch as a lighter alternative to Christmas pudding or instead of the traditional rich brandy butter. It is especially good served with meringues flavoured with ground ginger.

serves
6–8

4 eggs, separated
115g (4oz) caster sugar
1 teaspoon ground ginger
2 tablespoons brandy

425ml (15fl oz) double or
    whipping cream
6 large pieces stem ginger
    in syrup, chopped

Beat the egg yolks with the sugar, ground ginger and brandy. Whip the cream until it stands in soft peaks and add to the egg mixture. Whisk the egg whites until stiff and fold into the mixture. Pour into a lidded container and freeze for about 1 hour. Add 4 of the pieces of chopped stem ginger and stir evenly into the semi-set ice cream. Return to the freezer until completely set.

Scoop the ice cream into glasses, sprinkle with the remaining chopped ginger and pour over a little of the stem ginger syrup. Top with Chocolate Orange Sauce (see page 216) or Butterscotch Sauce (see page 219).

Ratafia Ice Cream

serves
6–8

115g (4oz) ratafia biscuits
150ml (5fl oz) sweet sherry
4 eggs, separated
85g (3oz) caster sugar
425ml (15fl oz) double or whipping cream
25g (1oz) chopped toasted almonds

Crush the ratafia biscuits and soak them in sherry for 20 minutes. Beat the egg yolks and sugar until thick and pale yellow in colour. Whip the cream until it stands in peaks and add to the egg mixture. Fold in the soaked ratafia biscuits. Whisk the egg whites until stiff and fold into the mixture.

Freeze in a lidded container for about 1 hour and then beat the mixture and add the chopped toasted almonds. Replace in the freezer and leave to set completely.

About 30 minutes before serving, move from the freezer into the refrigerator and leave to soften. Serve the ice cream topped with seasonal soft fruit and cream.

Clare College Mush

Also called Eton Mess, the original recipe for this traditional pudding is said to have come from Clare College, Cambridge. A delicious combination of strawberries, cream and crushed meringues, it can be flavoured with an orange- or berry-flavoured liqueur or vanilla essence. Other fruits work well – raspberries, and poached apricots, rhubarb, damsons and plums are favourites, but, best of all, I like a combination of strawberries and raspberries with a flavouring of liqueur and half cream and half yoghurt.

serves 6

2 large egg whites
55g (2oz) caster sugar
55g (2oz) icing sugar
225g (8oz) fresh strawberries
225g (8oz) fresh raspberries

1 tablespoon (plus an extra dash) raspberry liqueur
200ml (7fl oz) double cream
200ml (7fl oz) natural yoghurt

Preheat the oven to 110°C (225°F, Gas mark ¼). Whisk the egg whites until they form soft peaks, then beat in the caster sugar, a little at a time. Continue whisking for a further 10 minutes until the mix is smooth and shiny, then sift in the icing sugar. Spoon on to a sheet of non-stick baking paper arranged on a baking tray, then bake in the oven until dry, but with a slightly soft, chewy centre – about 2 hours. Remove from the oven and leave to cool on a wire rack.

When ready to assemble the pudding – and it is best eaten within 2 hours of making – cut the strawberries into halves or quarters, depending on their size, then toss with a dash of raspberry liqueur. Stir in the raspberries, reserving a few of the best ones for decoration.

Lightly whip the cream and yoghurt with a tablespoon of raspberry liqueur. Break the meringues into walnut-sized pieces and gently stir into the cream mixture with the fruit (don't overmix, because it looks very attractive with a raspberry-ripple effect). Spoon the mixture into glass dishes and serve chilled, decorated with the reserved raspberries.

Summer Pudding

The true old-fashioned Summer Pudding was made with raspberries and redcurrants only, but, if you wish, you can include small halved strawberries, white currants, blueberries, sweet, firm-fleshed cherries and a few blackcurrants – not too many of the latter or they will dominate the flavour of the pudding. If you are lucky enough to be able to get hold of some mulberries, they make a really delicious summer pudding, combined with half the amount of strawberries. Make sure you use good-quality bread.

serves
6

700g (1lb 9oz) fresh raspberries
200g (7oz) fresh redcurrants
115g (4oz) vanilla caster sugar or plain
    caster sugar
about 6 slices of day-old white bread,
    about 8mm (⅜in) thick
2 tablespoons raspberry liqueur

Put the fruit into a heavy saucepan and sprinkle over the sugar. Heat gently for 3–4 minutes only, until the sugar has dissolved and the juices have begun to flow. Cut the crusts off the bread and use it to line an 850ml–1.2l (1½–2 pint) pudding basin, bottom and sides. Overlap the slices slightly so that there are no gaps. Spoon the fruit into the basin, reserving a little of the juice for serving. Pour the raspberry liqueur over the fruit before finishing with a top layer of bread.

Put a plate on top that fits exactly inside the basin and weight it fairly heavily. Leave the pudding in the refrigerator overnight. Turn out just before serving and pour the reserved juice over any bread that isn't quite soaked through. Serve chilled with pouring cream or softly whipped double cream.

Floating Islands

This traditional Georgian pudding consists of a rich creamy custard, which is covered with poached meringues (the islands). It has a delicate flavour.

serves 6–8

600ml (1 pint) single cream
6 egg yolks
2 level teaspoons cornflour
175g (6oz) caster sugar
1 tablespoon rose water
850ml (1½ pints) milk, for poaching

1 vanilla pod
4 egg whites
pinch of salt
crystallized rose petals
toasted flaked almonds

Bring the cream gently to the boil in a heavy saucepan. Remove from the heat and cool a little. Cream the egg yolks, cornflour and 50g (1¾oz) sugar until almost white. Pour the hot cream over the egg-yolk mixture gradually, beating all the time. Rinse out the saucepan, leaving a film of cold water on the bottom. Return the custard to the saucepan and heat gently, stirring continuously until thick enough to coat the back of a wooden spoon (don't boil or the mixture will curdle). Remove from the heat and cool a little before stirring in the rose water. Strain into a shallow serving bowl, sprinkle with sugar and leave to cool.

To make the 'islands', fill a frying pan with milk, flavoured with a vanilla pod, and bring to simmering point. Whisk the egg whites with a pinch of salt until they stand in stiff peaks. Whisk in 115g (4oz) caster sugar gradually, until smooth and shiny. Remove the vanilla pod from the pan. Using a tablespoon rinsed in cold water between each addition, spoon 4 islands into the pan of simmering water. Poach on each side for 2–3 minutes, until firm. Remove each island and drain on a clean towel. Repeat until the meringue mixture is used up (about 8 islands). Leave to cool. Arrange the islands on the 'lake' of custard and chill. To serve, sprinkle with crushed crystallized rose petals and toasted flaked almonds.

Trinity Burnt Cream

Also known as Cambridge Cream or Trinity Pudding, this pudding was first introduced to Trinity College, Cambridge, by a Fellow in 1879 and served at dinner during May Week. It was brought in on a large silver dish and the caramelised top was cracked with great ceremony.

The recipe is said to have been based on an ancient Scottish dish, which may have been brought over from France by Mary, Queen of Scots. It is similar to the delicious French *creme brulée*. There are endless versions of this creamy pudding with different flavourings – lemon zest, vanilla pod or a bay leaf. The sugary top used to be browned by a 'salamander', a flat iron which was heated and passed over the top of the pudding. You can make this custard in one large baking dish or individual ovenproof dishes, and it is best made the day before you want to serve it.

serves
4–6

600ml (1 pint) double cream
1 vanilla pod, split lengthways
5 egg yolks
1 tablespoon caster sugar
about 4 tablespoons demerara sugar

Bring the cream with the vanilla pod very gently to the boil in a saucepan. Leave to cool a little, then remove the vanilla pod. Cream the egg yolks and sugar together in a basin until almost white. Pour the hot cream on to the yolks in a steady stream, whisking all the time. Strain the custard into a shallow 700ml (1¼ pint) ovenproof dish and then place it in a roasting tin filled with enough hot water to come halfway up the sides of the dish. Cook in a preheated oven, 150°C (300°F, Gas mark 2), for 1–1¼ hours or until just set.

Remove the dish from the oven and leave until cold. Chill in the refrigerator overnight, if possible. Just before serving, spread the demerara sugar in an even layer over the surface of the custard and spray with a little water (this helps caramelize). Heat a grill to its highest temperature, then place the pudding as near to the grill as possible until the sugar has melted and caramelized (if you have a chef's blowtorch, use this instead). Return the pudding to the refrigerator for 30 minutes before serving. Decorate with a few edible flowers (optional) and serve with a bowl of fresh cherries, strawberries or raspberries in season.

Devonshire Junket

This was a junket covered with clotted cream, popular in Devon and Cornwall – so simple, but so delicious. Junket has been made since the thirteenth century and is probably of Norman origin. Its name comes from the word *jonquette*, French for the little rush baskets in which it was made. The original junket was a rich confection of cream, curdled with rennet and flavoured with spices. Later, rose water and orange-flower water were added and junket was eaten alongside the jellies and flummeries at the end of a meal. It was traditionally served in beautiful junket bowls with stewed fruit but is especially good with fresh raspberries or strawberries.

 serves 4

600ml (1 pint) Jersey milk
  or single cream
1 heaped tablespoon caster sugar
1 tablespoon brandy

pinch of freshly grated nutmeg,
  plus extra for sprinkling
1 level teaspoon rennet
clotted cream, to serve

Heat the milk or cream to 38°C (100°F), then stir in the sugar to dissolve it, followed by the brandy, nutmeg and rennet. Stir well, then pour into a glass bowl or 4 individual serving dishes and leave to set at room temperature (not in the refrigerator), for about 4 hours.

Chill in the refrigerator for about 1 hour before serving plain or sprinkled with grated nutmeg and accompanied by clotted cream and soft fruit or a purée of fresh raspberries or strawberries.

Damask Cream

For a dessert that was popular in eighteenth-century Bath, make the junket using single cream rather than milk and omitting the brandy. Sprinkle the top with grated nutmeg. About 30 minutes before serving, mix together 4 tablespoons double or whipping cream, 3 tablespoons rose water and 1 tablespoon caster sugar. Pour this over the top of the junket. Serve with pink or red rose petals strewn over the top. Alternatively, mix 4 tablespoons clotted cream with the rose water and sugar and serve separately with the junket.

Mrs Beeton's Gooseberry Trifle

In this recipe, gooseberry pulp has replaced the more usual sponge cake at the bottom of the trifle, and is covered with a rich custard and topped with a 'whip', which was a Victorian version of syllabub. If possible, make the syllabub topping a day in advance. Any fruit pulp can be used.

serves
6

zest and juice of 1 lemon
6 tablespoons sweet white wine
   or sherry
2 tablespoons brandy
50g (1¾oz) caster sugar
600ml (1 pint) double cream

700g (1lb 9oz) green gooseberries
3 tablespoons cold water
250g (9oz) caster sugar
strip of lemon rind
4 egg yolks
1 level teaspoon cornflour

Put the lemon zest and juice in a small bowl. Stir in the wine or sherry, brandy and sugar until the sugar has dissolved. Cover and leave for several hours to infuse. Strain the liquid into a clean bowl and stir in 300ml (10fl oz) of the cream, gradually, beating until it almost reaches a soft-peak stage (don't use an electric beater – if overbeaten, syllabub will become grainy). Chill overnight.

Next day, top and tail the gooseberries and put them in a heavy saucepan with the water and 50g (1¾oz) sugar. Simmer gently for about 20 minutes until soft. Rub through a sieve or beat to a pulp. Add 175g (6oz) sugar – you may need more, if the gooseberries are tart. Put in a shallow serving bowl and leave to cool.

Bring the remaining cream slowly to the boil with the strip of lemon rind, and leave on one side to cool a little. Cream the egg yolks, cornflour and 25g (1oz) caster sugar together until almost white. Remove the lemon rind and pour on the hot cream in a steady stream, beating all the time. Rinse out the saucepan used for heating the cream, leaving a film of water in the bottom. Return the egg mixture to the pan and heat very gently until thick enough to coat the back of a wooden spoon (don't boil because the custard will curdle). Remove from the heat and leave to cool. Pour over the gooseberry pulp. Sprinkle with caster sugar to stop a skin forming and leave to get completely cold.

Pile the syllabub on top of the custard and chill well. Just before serving, decorate with twists of lemon rind or lemon slices and sprigs of fresh rosemary.

Old-English Sherry Trifle

for the base
1 fatless sponge cake made with
   3 eggs, 85g (3oz) caster sugar
   and 85g (3oz) plain flour or
   1 packet of trifle sponges
good-quality apricot jam or apple
   or quince jelly
115g (4oz) ratafia biscuits or
   macaroons
about 6 tablespoons medium
   sherry or Madeira
2 tablespoons brandy (optional)

for the custard
600ml (1 pint) single or
   double cream
1 vanilla pod, split in half
   lengthways
50g (1¾oz) caster sugar
2 teaspoons cornflour
6 egg yolks

for the topping
425ml (15fl oz) double or

Cut the sponge into 2.5cm (1in) slices and then liberally spread them with your chosen preserve. Arrange in a large glass bowl. Scatter over the ratafia biscuits or macaroons, then sprinkle liberally with sherry or Madeira and brandy, if using.

To make the custard, bring the cream with the vanilla pod to the boil. Mix the sugar with cornflour, add the egg yolks gradually and beat well until smooth. Remove the vanilla pod from the milk and pour on to the egg mixture, stirring all the time. Rinse out the milk pan, leaving a film of cold water in the bottom. Return the custard to the pan and stir well with a wooden spoon over a low heat until thick. Immediately the custard is thick enough, plunge the bottom of the pan into a bowl of cold water to stop the mixture curdling. Leave to cool a little.

When the custard is relatively cool, pour it over the sponge, and leave to cool completely. When cool, whip the cream until it stands in peaks and spread a thick layer over the custard. Pipe the top with the remaining cream and decorate with lots of crystallized fruits, nuts and extra ratafias – the more the merrier, especially at Christmas. In the summer, the trifle looks lovely decorated with crystallized flowers, rose petals or fresh edible flowers.

Apple & Brandy Trifle

for the base
1 fatless sponge made with
    3 eggs, 85g (3oz) caster sugar,
    85g (3oz) plain flour
    or 1 packet trifle sponges
about 6 tablespoons apple brandy

for the apple layer
3 large Bramley apples
3 Cox's apples
2 tablespoons light soft brown sugar
½ teaspoon ground cinnamon

for the custard
425ml (15fl oz) double cream

1 vanilla pod, split in half
    lengthways
2 large eggs
egg yolks from 2 large eggs
85g (3oz) caster sugar

for the cream topping
300ml (10fl oz) double cream
25g (1oz) icing sugar
vanilla extract to taste

for decoration
100g (3½oz) flaked almonds
25g (1oz) icing sugar
3 tablespoons apple brandy

Cut the sponge into 2.5cm (1in) slices and arrange them in a large bowl. Pour over the apple brandy and leave for at least 30 minutes to soak. To make the apple layer, peel, core and chop the apples. Place in a pan with the sugar and cinnamon. Cook over a medium heat until the apples are tender; leave to cool.

To make the custard, pour the double cream into a saucepan with the vanilla pod and bring to the boil. Meanwhile, mix the eggs, egg yolks and sugar together in a large bowl. When the cream reaches boiling point, pour it over the egg mixture, whisking continuously to prevent the eggs curdling. Strain through a fine sieve into a large bowl. Place over a pan of simmering water. Heat until the custard has thickened, whisking from time to time, then set aside to cool. Cover the soaked sponge with a layer of the apple mixture, then a layer of custard.

For the cream topping, whisk together the cream, icing sugar and vanilla until it forms soft peaks. Spoon on top of the custard. Mix the almonds, icing sugar and apple brandy together in a small bowl. Tip out on to a baking tray and toast in a preheated oven, 180°C (350°F, Gas mark 4), for 15 minutes, or until golden brown. Leave to cool, then scatter over the cream.

Lemon Meringue Pie

serves
6

for the pastry
175g (6oz) plain flour
1 tablespoon icing sugar
115g (4oz) cold butter, cut in
    small pieces
1 egg yolk
about 1 tablespoon ice-cold water

for the filling
115g (4oz) caster sugar
2 level tablespoons cornflour

grated zest of 2 large lemons
125ml (4fl oz) lemon juice
juice of 1 small orange
85g (3oz) butter, cut in small pieces
3 egg yolks
1 whole egg

for the meringue
4 egg whites, at room temperature
225g (8oz) caster sugar
2 level teaspoons cornflour

To make the pastry, sieve the flour and icing sugar together into a mixing bowl. Lightly rub in the butter, then add the egg yolk and enough water to mix to a dough. Knead briefly into a smooth ball, then roll out the dough and use to line a buttered 23cm (9in) loose-bottomed, fluted flan tin. Prick the base with a fork, line with foil and chill for 30 minutes to 1 hour or overnight. Put a baking sheet in the oven and preheat to 200°C (400°F, Gas mark 6). Bake blind in the usual way (see Apricot Amber Pudding, page 132). Remove from the oven and set aside. Lower the oven temperature to 180°C (350°F, Gas mark 4).

To make the filling, mix the caster sugar, cornflour and lemon zest in a medium saucepan. Strain and stir in the lemon juice gradually. Make the orange juice up to 200ml (7fl oz) with water and strain into the pan. Cook over a medium heat, stirring continuously, until thick and smooth. Once the mixture bubbles, remove from the heat and beat in the butter until melted. Beat the egg yolks and whole egg together, then add to the pan and return to the heat. Keep stirring vigorously for a few minutes until the mixture thickens and plops from the spoon. Remove from the heat and set aside.

Whisk the egg whites to soft peaks, then add half the sugar, a spoonful at a time, whisking between each addition without overbeating. Whisk in the cornflour, then add the rest of the sugar as before until smooth and glossy. Quickly reheat the filling and pour it into the pastry case. Immediately pile spoonfuls of the meringue around the edge of the filling (if you start in the middle, the meringue may sink), then spread so it just touches the pastry (to anchor it and help stop it sliding). Pile the remaining meringue into the centre, spreading so that it touches the surface of the hot filling and starts to cook, then give it all a swirl. Return to the oven for 18–20 minutes until the meringue is crisp.

Remove from the oven and leave to cool in the tin for 30 minutes, then remove the pie carefully from the tin and leave for at least another 30 minutes to 1 hour before serving. Eat the same day, or the meringue will be spoiled.

Chocolate & Prune Tart

Chocolate was introduced into Britain in the mid-seventeenth century from Mexico, where the Aztecs had mixed it with honey. It remained a luxury drink as long as the price of sugar was high and was never as popular as coffee or tea. A pie made with a chocolate filling like this would have been considered a great luxury.

for the sweet shortcrust pastry
175g (6oz) plain flour
pinch of salt
85g (3oz) icing sugar
150g (5½oz) unsalted butter
2 small egg yolks, beaten

for the prune purée
300g (11oz) stoned
    ready-to-eat prunes
2 tablespoons brandy

for the chocolate filling
100g (3½oz) good-quality plain
    chocolate (70% cocoa solids)
2 eggs, separated
300ml (10fl oz) double cream
85g (3oz) caster sugar
sifted icing sugar, to dust

To make the pastry, sieve the flour with the salt and icing sugar into a bowl. Rub in the butter, then mix to a soft dough with the egg yolks. Knead very briefly, then wrap the dough in clingfilm and chill in the refrigerator for about 30 minutes. Roll out and use to line a buttered 25cm (10in) flan tin. Bake blind in the usual way (see Apricot Amber Pudding, page 132).

Meanwhile, make the prune purée by simmering the prunes gently with barely enough water to cover, for 5–10 minutes or until very tender. Lift them out with a slotted spoon and process with the brandy and just enough of the juice to make a thick purée (about 3 tablespoonfuls). Spread over the base of the pastry case.

To make the chocolate filling, break the chocolate into pieces and place in a bowl, set over a pan of gently simmering water, making sure that the base of the bowl does not come into contact with the water. Remove the bowl as soon as the chocolate has melted and let it cool slightly before beating in the egg yolks, one by one. Lightly whip the cream and fold into the chocolate mixture. Whisk the egg whites until they form soft peaks, then sprinkle over the caster sugar and continue to whisk until glossy. Fold into the chocolate mixture, then pour into the pastry case.

Bake in the preheated oven, 200°C (400°F, Gas mark 6), for about 40–50 minutes until puffed up, set around the edges, but still wobbly in the centre. Serve the tart warm or cold dusted with icing sugar and accompanied by Vanilla Ice Cream (see page 202) or some whipped cream.

Basic recipes

Shortcrust Pastry

Shortcrust pastry is really simple to make. Use lard for a very short pastry or butter for a good flavour – or a mixture of the two, if liked. Solid vegetable fat and margarine can both be used for pastry making, but reduced-fat and low-fat spreads are unsuitable.

serves
4

300g (11oz) flour mixed with a
    generous pinch of salt
150g (5oz) lard, butter, or lard and
    butter mixed
6–8 tablespoons cold water

Put the flour and salt in a mixing bowl. Cut the fat into 1cm (½in) dice and add to the bowl. Using the tips of your fingers, lightly rub the fat into the flour until the mixture resembles fine breadcrumbs. Then add enough cold water to make a coherent dough – a little less or a little more than the quantity give above may be needed, depending on how dry the flour is.

Shape the dough into a ball that leaves the sides of the bowl clean, wrap in foil and chill in the refrigerator or put in a cool place for at least 30 minutes to rest before rolling it out on a floured surface and using.

Puff Pastry

Making *pâte feuilletée* (the true puff pastry of the French kitchen) requires both skill and time. This recipe is a simplified version, known in British cookery as 'rough puff pastry'. It won't rise as much as true puff pastry but is still good. Alternatively, puff pastry is easily available from the chill cabinets of supermarket freezers, either as blocks or as ready-rolled sheets. It makes the cook's life much easier. The fat must be cold from the fridge. Use a sharp knife to cut the pastry, and be careful not to crush the cut edges or get egg wash on them, or it won't rise as nicely.

serves 4

250g (9oz) flour, plus extra for
    working and rolling
175g (6oz) chilled fat (equal
    quantities of butter and lard)
iced water
salt

Put the flour in a bowl and add about ½ teaspoon salt. Using the coarse side of a grater, grate the butter and lard into the flour (dipping the fat into the flour periodically helps to make this easier). Once all the fat is in, start adding iced water, a tablespoon at a time, stirring the mixture with your hand until a stiff paste forms. Don't overdo the water: the mixture needs to be coherent but not sticky.

Turn on to a floured work surface and work for a moment, just enough to make sure the mixture is even. Then roll out into an oblong three times as long as it is wide; turn the top third down towards you and the bottom third up to cover this. Turn 90 degrees clockwise and repeat the rolling and folding process, then chill for 30 minutes. Repeat this rolling and folding process twice more, then give the pastry a final rest and it is ready for use. It can be made a day in advance, but if you do this, wrap it in foil or clingfilm and store in the fridge overnight.

Dumplings

Suet dumplings are comforting companions for a meaty stew, particularly one made with beef. They probably share a common ancestor with suet puddings, and are rib-sticking food intended to stretch precious supplies of other, more expensive ingredients. They are simple to make and easy to vary with different flavourings. Make the mixture just before you want to cook it. Plain flour mixed with 1 teaspoon baking powder can be used instead of self-raising flour if desired. The stew they are destined for needs to be completely cooked. Bear in mind that the dumplings will need about 25 minutes to cook after they have been added.

serves 4

115g (4oz) self-raising flour
60g (2¼oz) shredded suet
about 125ml (4fl oz) water, to mix
a pinch of salt

to flavour
1 generous tablespoon chopped parsley
  with a little thyme and marjoram;

or 1 generous teaspoon mustard powder and about 1 tablespoon chopped parsley or chives; or 1 generous tablespoon creamed horseradish; or a little chopped fresh tarragon

If you are reheating a stew, it is best to start this off before adding the dumplings. Put all the dry ingredients into a bowl. Add the flavouring ingredients if desired. Then add about two-thirds of the water and mix. The mixture should be fairly soft but not too sticky. Add a little more water if it seems dry. Form into balls the size of a large walnut and drop them on top of the stew.

If the stew is cooking in the oven, leave it uncovered after adding the dumplings. They will crisp slightly on top, and may colour a little in the heat. If the stew is cooking on the hob, drop the dumplings into the liquid and cover the pan.

Cook for a further 20–30 minutes in the oven at 180°C (350°F, Gas mark 4) until the dumplings are cooked through and slightly golden on top. Alternatively, allow about 20 minutes for a stew cooking on the hob.

For dumplings that are to be cooked on top of a stew in the oven, try replacing 40g (1½oz) of the flour with 40g (1½oz) dried breadcrumbs – this makes the surface crisper.

Chocolate Orange Sauce

350ml (12fl oz) water
115g (4oz) caster sugar
1½ tablespoons cornflour
25g (1oz) cocoa powder
1 tablespoon instant coffee granules
50g (1¾oz) good-quality dark
    chocolate
2 strips of orange zest
Grand Marnier to taste

This easy sauce can be stored in the refrigerator for 4 weeks to use on ice cream or any pudding whenever you fancy. Combine 200ml (7fl oz) water and the sugar in a saucepan. Bring to the boil, stirring occasionally to dissolve the sugar.

In a bowl, mix the remaining water with the cornflour and cocoa powder. When the sugar syrup is boiling, stir the cocoa mixture again and then pour it into the pan. Whisk very well, then simmer for 5 minutes. Add the coffee, chocolate and orange zest and stir until smooth.

Remove from the heat, cover and leave to cool completely. When the sauce is cold, strain it and flavour to taste with liqueur. Pour the sauce into a jar, cover and store in the refrigerator until needed.

Raspberry Sauce

225g (8oz) fresh raspberries
85g (3oz) caster sugar
juice of 1 lemon
2 tablespoons water

Heat all the ingredients in a saucepan over a very low heat. Simmer gently for 5 minutes. Rub through a sieve and taste for sweetness.

Butterscotch Sauce

55g (2oz) butter
150g (5½oz) demerara sugar
1 tablespoon golden syrup
150g (5½oz) evaporated milk

Melt the butter, then add the sugar and syrup. Stir until dissolved, then pour in the evaporated milk. Turn up the heat and beat until boiling. Serve hot.

Syrup Sauce

4 tablespoons golden syrup
2 tablespoons water
juice of ½ lemon

Simmer the golden syrup and water together in a small saucepan for about 2–3 minutes. Add the lemon juice and serve hot.

Vanilla Custard Sauce

6 large egg yolks
70g (2½oz) caster sugar
1 vanilla pod
300ml (10fl oz) full-cream milk
300ml (10fl oz) double cream

Beat the egg yolks and sugar together in a bowl until well blended. Split and scrape the seeds of the vanilla pod into a pan with the milk and cream and bring to the boil. Place the bowl over a pan of hot water and whisk the cream into the egg mixture. As the egg yolks warm, the cream will thicken to create a custard. Keep stirring until it coats the back of a spoon. Remove the bowl from the heat and serve warm or cold.

Cider Custard

2 large egg yolks
1 tablespoon cornflour
200ml (7fl oz) cider
2 tablespoons muscovado sugar
½ teaspoon ground cinnamon
400ml (14fl oz) double cream

In a small basin mix the egg yolks with the cornflour until smooth. Gradually add the cider, the sugar and the cinnamon. Pour into a saucepan and heat gently. Add the cream and whisk constantly over the heat until the custard has thickened.

Jam Sauce

3 tablespoons raspberry, strawberry,
    plum, apricot or blackcurrant jam
6 tablespoons water
1 teaspoon lemon juice

Melt the jam in a saucepan with water and lemon juice.
Push through a sieve to make a smooth sauce. Serve hot.

Lemon or Orange Sauce

4 tablespoons home-made lemon
    or orange curd
150ml (5fl oz) single cream

Mix the lemon or orange curd and cream together. Heat in a saucepan over a low
heat until hot but not boiling. Serve hot in a warmed jug.

Index

Numbers in *italics* refer to photographs